I Am Not a Poet

Written by Salonee Kumar

Illustrated by Anushka Dey
and Salonee Kumar

Layout Design by Rashi Shah

For the storytellers
whose stories
are untold.

Contents

Chapter One: Of Loss *and Learning*

Chapter Two: Of Love *and Healing*

Chapter Three: Of Letters *and Musings*

Preface

Step One: I tightly grip the nib of my pen.

Step Two: I pierce words into my journal until they rip the paper and repair my heart.

Step Three: I conclude with a ceremonious toss of my melodramatic monologue into the dustbin.

This is how I have been stringing together gibberish and calling it art since the age of five. A lot has changed over the years, but my writing process has remained the same.

I used to feel apprehensive about exploring the emotional complexities of my mind through art. Most of my work never saw the light of day because I dreaded criticism and the possibility of embarrassment. This sense of unworthiness was exacerbated during the Coronavirus pandemic when the world was isolated, frustrated, and grappling with unforeseen upheavals.

At the time, many people rediscovered their lost passions or discovered new ones. Some even managed to alleviate their anguish through writing. Unfortunately, the irony for writers dealing with depression is that when mental illness commandeers our minds, we cannot think straight. And so, for two years, I inadvertently swept everything under the rug of unconsciousness.

My thoughts were bottled up in my head, *and that is where I had to let them fester.*

I had to come to terms with the fact that words no longer flowed from my fingertips like a reservoir; I was parched. I became hesitant (and often mortified) to identify myself as a writer, an artist, or a poet.

And then, one night, as abruptly as I had stopped,
I began nourishing myself and my art again.

"Tonight, I wrote and wrote and wrote until my heart nearly gave out. I poured every feeling I've recently experienced into a pretty little cup, brimming over with lemon tea, ready to be sipped. Healing is hard, but writing makes it easier. I'm so excited about all the adventures I've promised myself I'll go on this year."

When I penned this journal entry in February 2023, I had an inkling of what I wanted my debut book to be about. However, I ended up writing *I Am Not a Poet* between 15th March and 15th May 2023[1].

The contents of this book reflect how I felt during those two months. I was at one of my lowest points, and I blotted my muddled emotions onto my safe haven— *paper*. I made space for my feelings and sat with them in silence every day.

I endeavoured to decipher them by translating them into my mother tongue—*poetry*.

I deliberated for a long time on whether or not to include certain anecdotes. After all, young adults are perceived as either too naive to understand heartbreak or too

---

1   With the exception of *New Beginnings* (a prose piece in Chapter Three) and my previously published works, which have been revised for better readability.

mature to recall childhood abuse. I am determined to challenge these narratives and welcome the spectrum of emotions we experience as we stand at the threshold of adulthood.

While writing *I Am Not a Poet,* it was important for me to stay true to myself and acknowledge all the feelings my soul harboured, even after the people they were meant for had left. I carried this sentiment forward as I embraced the chaos that characterises not only you and me, but also much of the world around us.

> Through loss, I have loved.
> Through stormy skies, I have painted rainbows.
> Through being silenced, I have found my voice.

Releasing the cold, inky blackness from my feather-quill heart onto scrap paper is liberating. I'm going to lie still as I let this feeling wash over me.

I am the product of amalgamations—
> Fierceness and docility.
> Strength and weakness.
> Love and hate.

Simultaneously, I am not defined by these dualities and contradictions.

The pieces in this book represent different layers of *my truths*—what my neurosis imagined to be real for me. I have never been able to separate truth from fiction, and this pandemonium makes it impossible for me to trust my own judgment and memory. But it also somehow captures my humanness—the vulnerable, sensitive, hostile, jealous, and traumatised sides of me. I believe that honouring all of them is the first step towards healing.

In using poetry as a medium for my recovery, I hope to create a space for you to validate your own memories. To know that you're not alone in feeling the way you do. To make non-linear progress in your own mental health journey, just like yours truly.

Solace found me when I wrote her letters: vulnerable, heartfelt, and brutally honest retellings of my experiences. Today, I wish to perform a dramatic reading of them for you. I will clamber onto a metaphorical stage, even as the little voice at the back of my mind tells me that I am not a poet.

Today, I will shut her out and open the windows.
Today, I will set myself free.
Today, I am a poet, and these are my stories.

I Am Not a Poet is a collection of my stories of loss, love, and letters. I now present them to you for your resonance and interpretation. I hope you uncover something that speaks to you and becomes uniquely yours, this World Mental Health Day[2].

All my love and hugs,
Sal (she/her).

2   The official book release for the first edition of *I Am Not a Poet* is on the 10th of October 2023. This date has been intentionally chosen as it coincides with the celebration of World Mental Health Day, which is organised by the World Federation for Mental Health (WFMH).

Content Disclaimer

My work delves into mature themes, and it is essential that my readers feel comfortable engaging with them. With this in mind, I kindly request that individuals under the age of 16 read *I Am Not a Poet* with care and precaution. Readers aged 16 and above, please note that you might also encounter content or illustrations that are unsettling. If you do find yourself feeling disturbed, I encourage you to take a moment to ground yourself. Please remember to prioritise your well-being and reach out to a trusted adult for any support you might need.

Trigger Warnings (TWs)

On that note, I would like to issue a trigger warning for graphic descriptions or subtle mentions of the following: death, suicide/self-harm (SH), sexual assault, physical violence, child abuse, alcoholism, bullying, mental illnesses, and eating disorders. The pieces that touch upon these subjects will be marked with a corresponding symbol at the top of the page, allowing you to skip them if necessary.

Symbol Guide

Note: I do not own the copyrights to these designs. They are commonly used by various organisations and individuals to visually represent the respective subject matter.

Identity and Context

I have intentionally *separated inspiration from creation* in the process of crafting my art. My narratives may appear to focus on specific individuals but actually encompass a range of different experiences. Therefore, I respectfully implore my readers to refrain from assuming the identities of characters or judging anyone based on these conjectures. There are no undertones of blame, shame, or guilt directed towards any real-life individuals, whether they pertain to others or myself. My aspiration is for this book to be acknowledged as a representation of *my subjective truths*.

To write
is to find
a refuge for your reflections,
a safe space for your senses,
a home for your heart.

Will you come with me
as I find
a refuge,
a safe space,
a home?

Chapter One:

Of Loss

and Learning

Welcome to My Canvas

Art is not conceived in the womb—
patiently nurtured
and eagerly awaited
for nine months.

    Art is the sharp blade
    that cuts through soft rays
    to bleed sunshine
    in the coldest ways.

And so,
to be an artist
is to lose
a piece of yourself
each time
you dare to bare
your words
for the world
to see,
to critique,
to do anything,
but accept.

    Welcome to my canvas.

The Nightmare in the Mirror

Everyone who knows me,
knows I dread horror movies—
they send chills down my spine
that regenerate themselves
in the middle of the night.

But how does the paranormal
form beads of sweat on my forehead,
when it is actually the normal
that looms over me like a warhead?

My heart is naked tonight.
It slips off its silk robe
and catches glimpses of itself
in the unforgiving glass
that I cannot ignore and pass.

Mirror, mirror on the wall,
why do I care about you at all?

The girl in the mirror looks at me,
eyes filled to the brim with hate—
red-hot fire burns up to her pupils,
as she bites her nails
and prepares to kill.

She throws the weight of her body
against the looking glass,
breaking the fourth wall,
and with it,
breaking my promise
never to get into a brawl.

She looks at me in spite—
her fuming smoke sets the stage
for a winnerless fight.

>She clenches her fists around my collar,
>tightening her grip by the second,
>to pull me into her grasp and holler,
>
>"How could you do this to me?
>To us?
>Just when I thought we were getting better?
>Is it because I look nothing like her?
>Why are you trying to be her?
>Am I not enough?
>
>Oh, and for hell's sake,
>can you stop overfeeding me,
>only to throw it all up later?
>Only to throw all our dreams
>out the window, you traitor?"

Her questions have me in a chokehold.
My dry throat gulps,
itching to comprehend them.

But this isn't a Socratic dialogue
where the questions lead to answers.

This is a children's cautionary tale.

Kids, don't be charmed
by the magic of words;
they are treacherous.

When you need answers the most,
words will abandon you
and become a ghost.

Language doesn't remember
its place on my lips,
the same way my body forgets mobility
upon seeing horror movie scenes—
a director's cut of my sleep paralysis
that I could not have foreseen.

> My mind books a one-way ticket
> to a trip through its own trail
> with tongue-tying twists and turns
> that made me sinister enough
> to envision my worst enemy
> to look exactly like me.

Except she's no longer a captive soldier.
She fights through the fractures
that have been poorly wrapped in gauze
for way too many years.

She screams like a blemished banshee
warning of her own impending death,
and calls for what's rightfully hers—
Treatment.
Better treatment.

> The nightmare in the mirror
> is a fever dream
> that dribbles into reality.

She is a horror movie I never want to see,
for she makes me consider the possibility
that the line between the real and the reel
is blurrier than ever,
and I'm left to wonder
if she's my worst nightmare
or I, hers.

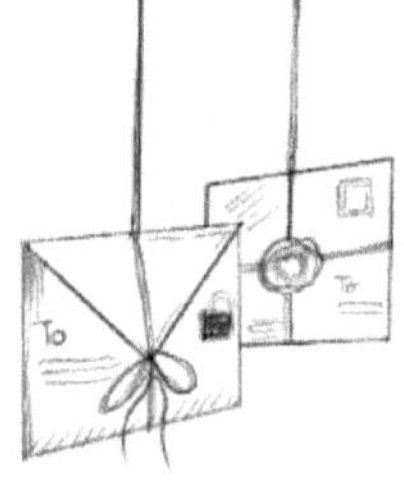

Scarlet Letters

The Libran letter you wrote
was enclosed in an envelope
addressed to my name,
but the letters were looped in a language
my eyes could not read,
and I was to blame.

I borrowed a dictionary,
tracing my tremoring fingers
along the translation columns,
only to see her scrawled notes
in all the margins.

I slammed the book shut
and let the dust settle into my lungs,
before swiftly hurling my fists
at the library wall—
cracked cement
on the tip of its Scarlet tongue.

It was the same colour as the letters
you had the nerve
to creaselessly[1] crumple and chew.
But I had to leave
without a smoking gun,
conceding that I could not incriminate you.

My love is not your consolation prize.
My love won't tolerate
the red herrings in your eyes.

---

1   I have attempted to play on the words 'crease' and 'ceaselessly'.

I hope the silk on her sheets
entangles you in her thread of lies,
and she torments your nightmares,
where, in your two-forked tongue,
your secret language dies.

    I had a dream
    where she picked up the quill
    to write a letter too.
    Infidelity dribbled
    down her ink-pot mouth,
    as her blue-stained tongue
    spat on your shoes.

    She wore them
    when she ran to the mailbox
    and addressed the envelope to your name,
    but knew the receiver was another pawn
    in her covert chess game.

It takes two to tango,
but we had four left feet,
while her agile Gemini double-crosses
enthralled the viewers in a sold-out stadium
where we had booked the front-row seats.

It's funny that you'll never see
she and I are more alike
than you make us out to be—
putting on a show for the world,
only to receive dead roses at our feet.

A Vandal's Tantrums

I begged for a morsel of your love,
throwing temper tantrums
like a neglected child
who was hurting
and hurting everyone around.

But you weren't around.

So, how was I supposed to know
that drawing with crayons on the walls
doesn't create a masterpiece;
it just leaves indelible marks
with no one to take the fall?

I started painting a portrait
of you and the woman you enshrined,
then stepped back to take it all in,
but the figure next to you wasn't mine.

You said you never cried
after calling it quits with me,
but upon *her* rejection,
conjured up a surging sea.

I was right to be worried.
I knew exactly what you did.

*My fragile hands barely held on
to a bucket much larger than me.*

I tried to repaint,
neat and slow,
failing miserably
to fill in the lines and gaps,
so I made myself let you go.

    The weight on my shoulders
    evaporated into thin air,
    as I tied up all the loose ends
    into a risky rope to swing from,
    and bolt faster than lightning
    from a silent demon's lair.

On Trial

Your sincerest apologies
swept me off my feet.
Little did I know you'd break them
the last time that we'd meet.

You salted my wounds,
finely garnishing them
with a dash of lemon zest.
Now, a moth sits on my knee,
devouring your insults on my body.

    Actions speak louder than words,
    but you were speechless
    while squandering both.
    Well, the court is now in session,
    so you can take your oath.

When men commit a felony,
they never have *mens rea*—
they are innocent until proven guilty.

But how do I prove
something adds up in moot,
when my brain is wired such
that numbers aren't my strong suit?

    My lack of admissible evidence
    made me imprison myself
    and lock up my rational thoughts
    that expressed themselves
    in irrational retorts.

I put you on a pedestal for so long—
the same one from which
your lawyers swayed everyone,
leading them to believe
you could do no wrong.

 Loving you was like being on trial,
 questioning whether I got it right,
 or if my gut experienced turbulence
 on a plane that never took flight.

Why did our voices
speak volumes of fury,
after everything
we quietly told the jury?

Our lawsuit has no winner—
just a prolonged verdict
that makes my patience grow thinner.

 You have made me realise
 the value of fidelity
 and emotional availability—
 of a partner who won't shut down,
 but openly communicate with me.

I want to forget you exist,
erasing the blackboard of my brain
like Clementine
from *Eternal Sunshine of the Spotless Mind*—
two borderline personalities
charting the cartography
of their own border lines.

And one day, I will succeed
in leaving behind
the remnants of you
on the same benches,
where, across corridors,
you used to watch me read.

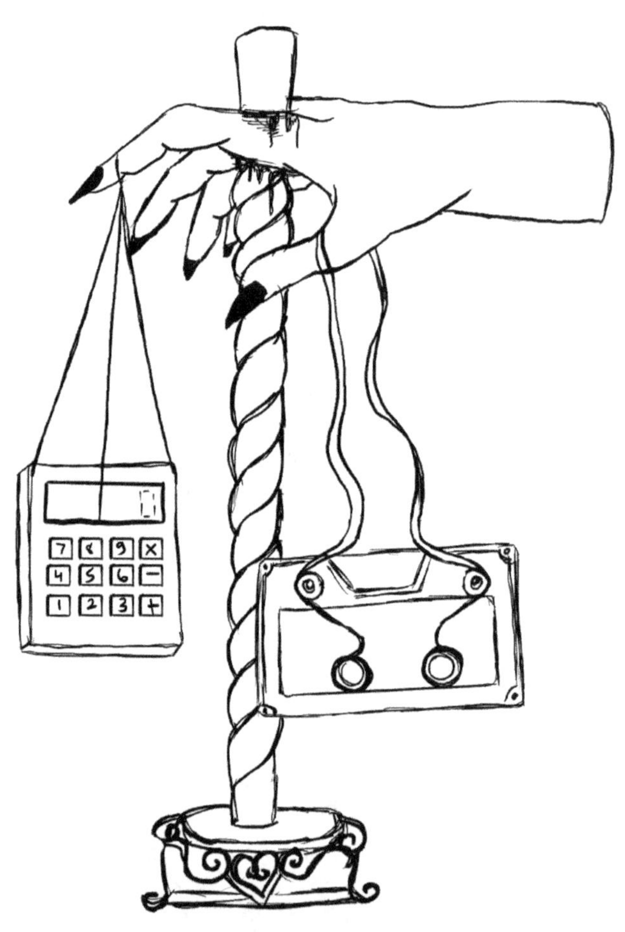

Passenger Seat

You're long gone,
but the memories of you have stayed
like the lingering scent
of my perfume in your car—
a mist of floral air,
now forever decayed.

I see us in a reel
bounded by 16 mm film,
which isn't a lot,
but we still try so hard
to get it right in one shot.

We enact a playful scene
of me gently tucking
Raat ki Rani behind your ear
because it's the only flower
you said you held dear.

You were a ray of golden sunshine
back when I could still call you mine.

You'd nuzzle your face
into your golden retriever's ears
and shine warmth on my skin
to dry up my residual tears.

I used to melt at what I'd see
and think to myself,
"This is exactly how I want
my future Sundays to be."

That future is as unimaginable
as us being together now,
for I carried heavy baggage
from my past travels—
*survivalist tendencies
that weighed us down.*

These overpacked suitcases
with outdated labels,
unknowingly taught me
to believe false fables.

My passport got banned
and I was sent out in exile—
*an immigrant in my homeland
that spread out for miles.*

    I vowed never to travel the world again.
    But then, you sent me a plane ticket.

    You took me stargazing,
    and through the telescope,
    I saw a universe of possibilities.
    My eyes lit up as they saw
    how we sat in silence with ease.

That's when you wove
feathers and dreams
on your shoulder
to give my heavy head a pillow.

But the night grew colder.

I saw my trust issues printed out
in a newspaper rather absurd—
"What if someone else
is sleeping in the same bed,
and *you* just haven't heard?"

You shrugged it off
as a baseless tabloid
and handed me my room keys;
I could rest in peace.

> I wish the universe had conspired
> against my unresolved fears,
> which never let me believe you—
> even when there was no one else in sight,
> even when I slept perfectly fine each night.

> *I am sorry for not healing enough*
> *to let you treat me right.*

I have set out once again
to look out the window
while crossing the Arabian Sea,
singing along to James Arthur
on a ride I thought you'd take with me.

You see, I got my driver's license,
and can relate to every word
in Olivia Rodrigo's song,
because I, too,
still hear your voice in the traffic—
we're laughing over all the noise[1].

---

[1]   The last two lines of this stanza are direct references
to the song 'drivers licence' by Olivia Rodrigo. The spelling
variations stem from different grammatical rules in American
and British English, respectively.

Except this time,
I hear static noises
crooning off-beat,
as I sit all alone
in my driver's seat.

Panic Attack

My soul craves peace,
and yet,
it ignores my desperate cries
to find a healthier release.

It persists in doubling
my rib cage as a ladder,
climbing
for hours
and hours
and hours
until my dandelion thoughts scatter.

It makes me, a control freak,
lose control of my breath,
sending thundering jolts
that shock my organs,
scaring me half to death.

It renders me an electric pole
as I stand alone
in the godforsaken monsoon,
shivering to my last bone.

But as soon as I think
the current has passed,
I stumble off the rollercoaster,
processing the nosedive
that made my stomach freefall.

My arms cross over my trembling legs
to steady them as I hide my face—
as if I can really bury myself at will
because it feels like my anxiety
has the feral power to kill.

> Tears saturate my body with guilt,
> as I float over it like a ghost,
> to watch from above
> *how I hollowed out*
> *the man I loved the most.*

He would gently cradle
my shaking body close—
a tender and kind understanding,
as I stutteringly apologised
for how I always froze.

But he wouldn't hear any of it,
reassuring me it wasn't my fault,
slowly counting down with me,
starting over and over,
until my breath synced with his.

And when it did,
he traced his fingers along my neck,
and endearingly asked
if I wanted a forehead kiss.

> *He loved me hard*
> *on the days I felt hard to love,*
> and shielded me from myself
> when my anxiety pushed and shoved.

He's gone now,
and I understand why—
his bright, blue sky could only be clear
when my dark thoughts learned to fly.

They have grown
terribly repulsive wings,
dotted in all the shades
of all the colours I hate.

But I won't sever them,
for healing still counts—
even when it looks hideous
and enmeshed in hate,
even when it has caressed my skin
over a year too late.

    I see a bird swoop down
    to take respite from her flight,
    and nurture her unhatched eggs
    in the plum of the night.

    As this vision
    quickly disappears,
    my vision
    slowly clears.

My mind brings me back
to the gift of the present.

I may never find sunshine
in human form again,
but some creatures are meant to thrive
in the murky corners of a den.

And in my comfortably deserted nook
at the spirals of a forgotten tree,
my soul will count down
with my impotent body,
until it finally sets my breath free.

Your Waves Come Ashore

If I had a grain of sand
for each time I repeated,
"I want to go to the beach
right outside your door",
I could build sandcastles
on my own damn shore.

    But my rage didn't start out this way.
    You see, I once used to say,

    "I see oceans in your eyes—
    turquoise blue
    with limitless days to seize,
    ebbing in,
    and flowing out,
    as you so please.

But your contact leaves me
with a sinking feeling
that you will soon decide
it's time to ripple away.

    So, I wait.
    I wait for the moon,
    in all her glimmering glory,
    to bring your tides
    a *little* closer to my sand.
    I wait for you to open the jar
    of seashells encrusted
    by these very hands."

Your waves were tantalising,
feeling out all my feelings,
but it was too much.
I was too much.

    So, you left.
    You left me with dampened hopes,
    until the sun's rays
    seared through my wounds,
    drying me into cracked clay.

I used to wait
for your waves to come ashore,
but now,
the tides will be low forevermore.

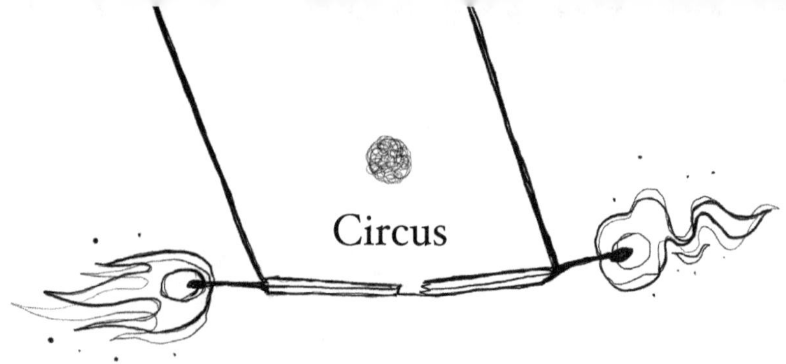

Circus

Our twin flame came down
to how we burned each other down—
ringmasters playing with fire
that could set ablaze a whole town.

I was a clown for wishing
things would go back to the start—
as if I could jump through flaming hoops
to fix what we knew had fallen apart.

Your actions,
or a lack thereof,
weighed heavy on my chest.
So, I churned out poetry,
turning the breathlessness
of my panic attacks
into mediocre art at best.

I painted my face
so you'd finally call me
an artist,
and rhythmically swung
over and under,
above and around
imaginary ropes in a circus
where you were the only audience.

I made a fool of myself,
trying to make you laugh,
trying to get you
to get the hints.

I suppose that's where I made my first mistake.

    I wondered if you were at a different circus
    or had abandoned the art altogether,
    for I had been left at the trapeze before
    and my legs were starting to get sore.

The Art of Loving

I penned you a sappy poem
the very first time I saw you,
but you couldn't read the word *'no'*
even when I wrote it five times
in your favourite shades of blue.

Nothing could melt
the wax I sealed alone,
not even your crocodile tears
over the phone.

You left my lake of letters stagnant—
a breeding ground for mosquitoes
in envelopes unsealed,
thriving in the puddles
of emotions concealed.

A slow-burning
learned helplessness
trained me to go with the flow,
letting my ink-stained hands ache,
and my poems take the blow.

They numbed me like anaesthesia,
so I'd overlook the agony
we called affection,
and forget that you'll forget me
when this drug wears off,
only to reveal an insidious infection.

Each and every time
I strived to sit and mend,
my exhausted heart
wanted to bring us to an end.

You read my mind for once
and did it by yourself;
you knew I couldn't let go
of the stories on my bookshelf.

    I was a proud storyteller,
    and all I wanted to do was write
    poems replete with clichés and syntax errors
    to read aloud to my own mirror.

    I didn't want to condense them
    into digestible haikus,
    just so my words didn't overwhelm
    or give you the blues.

So now,
I write soliloquies
that only make sense
in my strange little mind—
the same one you once fell in love with,
but now, with space impossible to find.

    I hope I have finally given
    the avoidantly attached child in you
    all the space he needs,
    because the anxiously attached girl in me
    is taking up space
    after being freed.

She is writing books you'll never read
about people you'll never meet,
and that is the art of loving
without missing a beat.

The Garden of Eden

I thought we were building
the Garden of Eden—
grazing pastures to feed in
and lush love to bear fruits,
but you didn't feel the same,
and yanked us by the roots.

　　　I want to say it was because
　　　I blew out the candle
　　　like an overexcited kid,
　　　or that you didn't plan
　　　harvests and spring celebrations
　　　the way Demeter and I did.

　　　Or maybe I was fated
　　　to conceal the bite of a snake—
　　　the venomous mark
　　　of true love gone fake.

We tried to plant the seeds of love,
but the weeds of resentment grew dire.
My words unsaid
heaped up in my journal—
a pile of dried leaves
waiting to catch fire.

And so, it lit,
but without a spark.

We had lost the spark.

Which Galaxy Is
Ours to Burn?

The only time you looked at me
was when our eyes were closed,
and I felt my heart suffocate
when fleeting thoughts of letting go
were peacefully unopposed.

    You were never ready for a relationship,
    and I was never ready to let you flee—
    desperately clinging onto breadcrumbs,
    honoured to even be a ninth priority.

I still pick fights with you,
picking you apart
for all the excuses and secrets
I was last to know.

I still encrypt messages in bottles—
ones that won't reach your waves—
about how you never seem to grow.

    But each time my tongue curls up
    to roll your name out,
    I bite it,
    slurping the curse word back in,
    quieting the voices
    that murmur in my ears,

    "Are you challenging the universe
    to battle you in a duel?

Or are you imploring it
to throw you a bone,
so you can bury him in the cemetery
of your what-ifs and forlorns?"

I'm going to let the universe decide
which galaxy is ours to burn.
And if it's not in this multiverse,
we'll fuel through the woodsmoke passion
immortalised in my final verse.

Thirteenth

I saw the thirteenth coming,
for I had a list
of reasons to leave
just the same.
But when our prophecy came true,
I convinced myself
I was entirely to blame.

    Salt drizzled down
    my textured face—
    raining,
    pouring,
    tearing up into a void
    where I idealised you
    and lost myself.

    I inhaled paracetamols
    as if you would vanish
    with my throbbing headache,
    and the last year would dissolve
    into your maroon hoodie
    the way I did on sad days.

I get déjà vu
each time I see that guy
who looks just like you.
But he's not the face
I keep in my locket,
or the love interest of the poems
folded in my pocket.

Many fear the number thirteen,
but I feared not having the courage
to tell you I deserved more.
I needed to stop defending
why your waves sparsely came ashore.

All I ever wanted
was a lover who expressed their love,
and spoke to me at least once a day—
like the sun that never fails to rise
when the moon says her goodbyes.

All you ever did
was slowly phase me away
until my crescent smile faded
like our starless city sky.

All we ever had
was a tactile tenderness
too far away for me
to touch,
to have,
and to hold.

Each time you used
the   distance
to justify your distance,
you resembled a stranger
who could walk past me
as if they didn't know
my body was the collateral damage
in the collision between
my head and my heart.

You see, our door was delivered
without instructions—
I would push
and you would pull,
like star-crossed lovers
crossing each other,
meeting neither's needs in full.

    I miss you,
    but I don't miss the butterflies
    anxiously fluttering their wings
    and getting sucked into a whirlpool
    of perennially invisible strings.

    After all, making time for me,
    and your promised therapy,
    were obligations remembered
    only after my incessant pleas.

I was tired of you and me.
But I was never tired
of what we could have been.

    I'm grateful for all the thirteenths
    we gleefully spent together—
    playing you Taylor Swift's songs,
    explaining the significance of this number,
    and how she's been my favourite for so long.

    Or all the thirteenths
    I embraced your family and friends
    who cared for me as one of their own.
    I thank them for the kindness they've shown.

I recall how your mother
interwove her love
into crochet sunflowers—
a soft, sweet affirmation
that I would blossom
with her dear sun ahead.

And then, the sun set on our love,
darkness collapsing all around
the virtual house you built
just for future us.

I really tried to understand
when rare dinner dates
turned into eating separately
because you had so much on your plate.

But deep down, we knew
the timing for you and me
was always just a little too late.

Even after all this time,
I wish I had cured your last scar—
the worst one that gashed your heart—
silently and from afar.

Believe me,
I wanted to show I care,
but I should've known
you didn't want to share.

I am sorry it had to be that way.
I am learning and doing better today.

It has only been a few days,
but I feel all the stages of grief at par.
Sunsets wear a different shade of magenta—
even the sky mourns that you're so far.

But I am doing my best to move on,
and praying that both of us
will be okay by dawn.

Graveyard Flower

In the greatest love stories I've read,
and the romantic comedies I've been spoonfed,
why do the lovesick soulmates
always meet sickly tragic fates?

My mud-caked hands toiled
to build something special
in the midst of a mess,
brushing back sweaty strands
to make it all look effortless.

But you ignored my presence
while standing over the cornerstone,
nonchalantly pouring cement around—
all while I was crumbling underground.

The stench of blood draws in
maggots who stealthily crawl,
mocking the heartsick who carry flowers
to charm the ghosts that roam these walls.

They say home is where the heart is,
but does the drunk know his way back home?
Tripping on uneven sidewalks,
slurring his speech,
pleading with strangers for directions—
the drunk doesn't know what home is.

My house now stinks
of your sneers and beers.

My clock's hands have straightened up
to strike twelve on the wall.
With each stroke, I ponder,
how, from grace,
even angels inevitably fall.

And I had the tragic luck
of having Lucifer fall for me.

    I wish we had said
    goodbye for good
    the very first time you absconded.
    But you charmed your way back in,
    and left me in captivity
    to believe we'd finally bonded.

I suppose all my labour merited
was an unsold, drooping flower,
sheltered in yesterday's newspaper—
half-solved puzzles in smudged ink,
gone, just like us,
in four eyes' blinks.

Clean

They say hair holds memories,
so I impulsively chopped mine off,
hoping my tresses would forget
the feeling of your fingertips
entangling their matted threats.

 I recently read an article—
 'It takes less than a month
 for skin cells to renew'.
 So, I started showering thrice a day,
 scrubbing out the hearts you drew
 all around mine in May.

I stopped playing lawn tennis
and stowed away my keyboard—
backhand strokes
fade into the background,
and chord progressions regress
without a single sound.

 My muscle memory has amnesia—
 it dismisses the story
 of how I learned to breathe
 only after collapsing from anoxia.

I remember and I forget,
I forgive and I regret—
no matter what I choose,
I end up feeling upset.

I suppose I should be grateful
because my eyes don't know
what they've seen.

There's so much
I don't write about
because it's all been wiped clean.

      I only wish you were on that list,
      because despite my shorter hair
      and newly polished skin,
      you are etched into my memories
      like the only one who exists.

Projection

My deepest fears rule the Underworld,
Cerberus guarding the trapdoor to my heart—
snarling at anyone who tries to enter,
and glaring at anyone who dares to leave.

> Jealousy took a heavy toll
> when it gnawed at my soul—
> a price I paid in partners lost,
> bridges burned
> each time I felt crossed.

> I projected my insecurities
> like a beacon of light—
> a tower house warning passersby
> of unwarranted suspicions
> in plain sight.

But why wouldn't I have felt inferior?
I had nothing at all—
just a girlhood of adjectives
like *fat* and *ugly*
spray-painted on my graffiti wall.

I was instructed to hold my head high
only to venerate skinny girls
who stood higher.

> I was painfully aware
> of the hurt I caused,
> and blissfully unaware
> of the dirt in my own claws.

To all the women
I was ingrained to view
as competition
before companions,
I am sorry.

    It was never actually about them,
    but I still wielded
    an axe of mayhem,
    chopping through
    when they cheered,
    until my mind finally cleared.

    But was it really clear,
    when my self-worth
    was commanded
    by constructed fears?

    And the fear of what?
    That I was not smart or hot?
    Or that a woman
    seemingly better than me,
    would make my lover see in them
    everything I couldn't be?

I sit at this rusted door
of unseemly feelings,
and furiously unhinge it
only to find
that everyone is hiding something
behind their corroded doors
and their taped-back hinges.

I have this sinking feeling
that our vessels will sink into the earth,
but our stories will remain afloat
in the boats of those dearest to us.

    I start repairing this cracked shelf,
    scratching out pictographs
    as ancient as patriarchy itself.

We are wild animals in a cage,
pitted against each other
to eat the submissive one alive—
suffering excruciating pain
to temporarily entertain.

Our world manufactures insecurities,
selling them in pretty diet pill bottles
and on riskless surgery tables,
immobilising women's bodies
for 'trends' that aren't even stable.

    It is in this world
    that I long for my envy
    to retract into the attic
    like a forgotten ghost.
    But how my appendage
    strives to flee
    is not palpable to most.

    My loved ones know, but can't say
    how the commotion in this bedlam
    compounds by the day.

I push to resolve it
in the strands of my hair,
but pulling them out, one by one,
cannot answer my prayer—
"I don't want my toxicity to worsen.
I just want to be a better person."

    This chase for perfection
    makes my heart go fast.
    But is it adrenaline,
    or the hysteria of a race
    where I end up dead last?

    Who entered me in this competition?
    Why is losing a sin?
    And how can I call myself a feminist,
    when my heart is a splintering schist?

I'm violently reconstructing myself
from the very metamorphic rock
that wore me down,
no longer waiting for a narcissist
to fashion me a secondhand crown.

I detest the brute I turned into,
so I'm ruthlessly executing her.
I've decided I'm through.

    Another woman's success
    is not my failure,
    but a path paved for generations
    of fellow sisters,
    so delightful and dear—
    just like the women before us,
    and the ones to come after.

I will project her success
onto a cinema screen—
celebrating her loudly,
crowning her a queen,
*and being a true feminist
by unlearning what I've seen.*

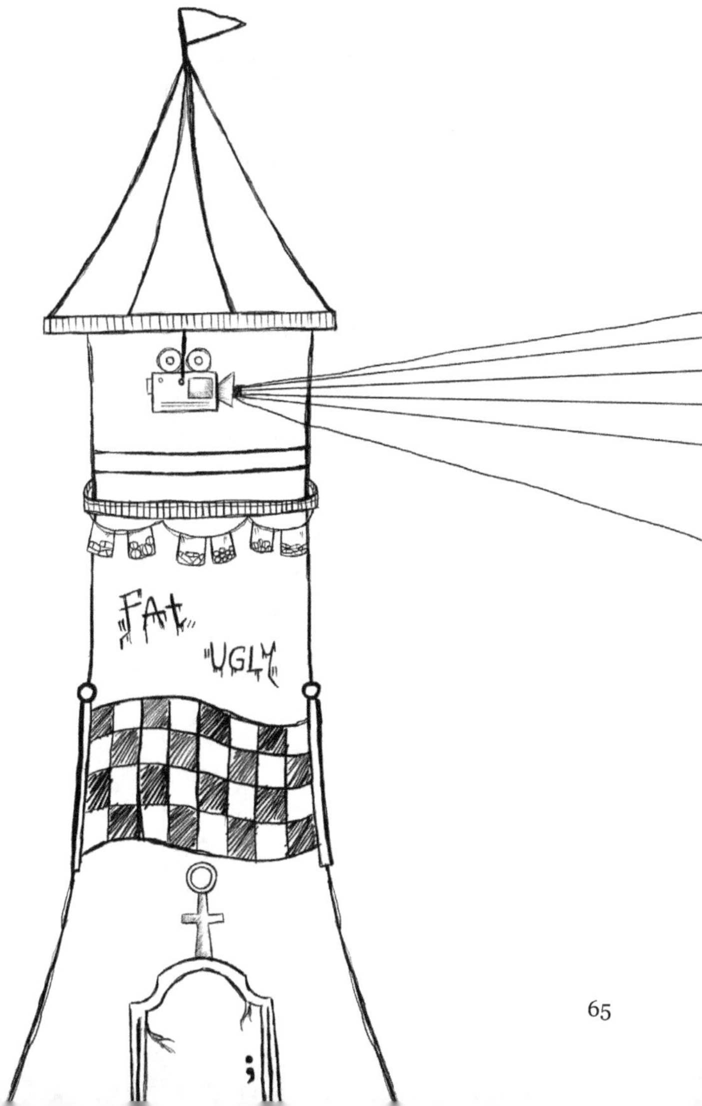

If Only

First published in *Tartan 2019*—the annual magazine of
Bombay Scottish School, Mahim, Mumbai.

A few months ago,
I visited the graveyard
to see someone
I hadn't met in a while.

> As I bent down to touch
> the smooth, freshly laid stone,
> my heart almost tore apart,
> and tears rolled down my cheeks
> to the tomb of the girl
> who deserved to smile.

There was only a row
of jagged leaves on a vine
entwined around her grave.

The world had left my friend
with *nothing*
but this.

> Beneath the moss
> in an orderly line,
> I saw a little flower,
> choked by the thorns
> growing above it amiss.

I picked up the gentle thing.
Though then November,
it was bound to bloom
by early spring.

The flower was tiny,
dull yellow,
almost too frail.
But it was gently curved
over the edge of a leaf
with great detail.

I took it home
and placed it in an ordinary glass.
With water and a little sunshine,
I let it grow.

December, January, and February
had all passed.
And then, the flower bloomed;
it no longer hung down low.

I felt like the proud parent
of a young child.
Watching my beautiful flower
sway in the breeze,
I smiled.

Suddenly, I felt an ache
somewhere inside,
and my bottled-up emotions
poured out as I cried.

The little flower said so much,
though it spoke not a word.
If only that fearful night,
my friend's cry for help
had been heard.

Mummy Tells a Lie

First published in *Tartan 2017*—the annual magazine of
Bombay Scottish School, Mahim, Mumbai.

Mummy, mummy, ask I must,
why are that man's hands bleeding red?
Oh, why is he covered in dust,
as he rests on the street
without a bed?

    Oh, mother, why do I see
    a little girl cooking,
    her eyes welled up with tears,
    instead of going to school with glee,
    and enjoying herself with all her peers?

Dear mamma, will you tell me why
the soil is so cracked and dry?
And why, in the straw-roofed hut,
does that farmer cry?
Is it because his crops seem to die?

    Mommy, do tell me,
    Why is uncle bruised and scarred all around,
    as he creeps under the rusty, electrified fence
    to see his comrades, on the other side,
    sleeping on the ground?

And mother, I want to know
why that boy is hanging from a rope,
as he sleeps while standing,
his face looking low;
dreaming on a cot, could he not cope?

My mummy held my hand
and gave me a smile so sad.

    "Fear not, the world is a place not bad,
    and all of these are simply God's beautiful creations",
    she said as we walked on by.

But I have this lurking feeling
that mummy, for once,
tells a lie.

Caged Freedom

First published in *Tartan 2015*—the annual magazine of
Bombay Scottish School, Mahim, Mumbai.

Sometimes, when I look up at the sky
and catch a glimpse of a bird or two,
I wonder how they smoothly fly,
ever so easily, cutting through the blue.

Sometimes, when I hear a crow crowing,
its smooth, black feathers glowing,
or find a wild turkey
with feathers grey and murky,
or see a peacock dancing,
its magnificent colours enhancing—
I sit and wonder,
have we humans committed a blunder?

Circling above our heads each day,
begging us not to make them our prey,
for even a single stroke of an arrow
can make death meet an innocent sparrow.

How beautiful these creatures are—
singing like angels,
shining like stars.

But, ah, they compare to none
when they hear the firing of the gun,
for the creature I deemed free, lays dead,
trapped in the greedy hunter's clever thread.

Birds are either caged or free,
but the difference,
do note,
is easy to see—
the free bird sings not with fright,
while the caged one silently cries at night.

Holding Hands With Death

When the zephyr dances 'cross white wisps
to the pulse of my heartbeat,
and the silence is tinted with the cadence
of faint fights on the street,
the slab feels wetter beneath my feet.

My body quivers over an invisible wire,
proving my nimbleness to Zeus,
requesting to be rewarded
with electric flashes and striking abuse.

    I beckon my beloved friend
    by holding out my hand,
    "Drop by the next time
    you dip your toes in Bombay sands.
    Then, you can take me away with you
    to a land where I can start anew."

But does Death listen? No.
She passionately grazes my wrist,
leaving behind concealed scars
that are only occasionally kissed.

Death makes me romanticise
a ghost that should leave me aghast.

    Death is not beautiful,
    or peaceful,
    or freeing.
    She carries with her a basket
    woven from the pain
    of every human being.

She is both,
a smitten lover
planning a wedding,
and a bitter enemy
plotting revenge.

Death is a living constant,
knelling to mark her presence,
as she holds my shivering hands
through the lively sunlit mornings
and undying moonlit crescents.

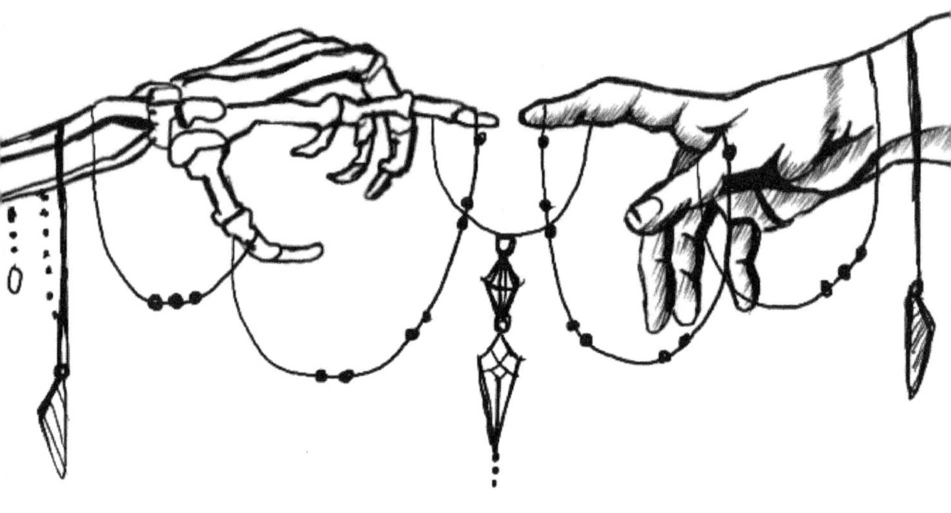

Note: The concept for this art was inspired by the renowned fresco painting, *The Creation of Adam*, by Michelangelo.

The Loss of Grief

Grief steadily crept up
like an ivy vine
on a dilapidated building
when it first hit me
that I'd lost my home—
like I ever even had the key.

I was just another brick on the wall,
squished between layers of cement
I could not concretely call
safe,
mine,
home.

But Grief heard my muffled thoughts
and gave each of them a voice,
*so she could teach me the difference
between sound and noise.*

Grief ensnared within me
all that dared to grow
beneath her,
and all that managed to grow
despite her.

Grief made my labyrinthine mind
screech into the void,
"He loves me,
he loves me not,
he loves me..."

Knot.

And, in an instant,
Grief sent shivers
down my bent spine.
He loves me not.

    How could he possibly love me
    when my roommate
    perches on my shoulder,
    warning all those with open arms
    never to enter?

At an age when I could
barely open my eyes,
I convinced myself it was *I*
who reeked of alcoholic lies.

    Grief has carved a hole in my bones,
    and nestled into her newfound home.

    She unveils the curtains
    as if nothing transpired,
    and sunlight is a visitor
    only on the days she is tired.

It's tricky to open up the doors
Grief paranoidly locked up;
I'm scared to let her go.
I have sought solace in her;
she hasn't tried to leave
like everyone else I know.

Perhaps, I have yet to learn
how to grieve
the loss of Grief.

Catch-22

Thrilling is my affair with words
that keeps my insanity at bay.
But it is this very madness
that makes you listen
to what I have to say.

And yet, there are stories
I will never be ready
to stand in a room
and fearlessly read aloud.

So, I switch the microphone off,
and come face-to-face
with a disappointed crowd.

My brain replays...

The torture that broke
my developing back;
it involved a terribly abusive
suitcase drill.

The birthday I witnessed
another's attempted suicide;
I was forced to watch
while standing still.

I can hear my heart
thud right out of my chest.
I'm trying to write,
but I can't give them my best.

There is harmony in hate,
as my organs take swings
to finish what he started—
taking over as kings
and pushing against me
like they remember he once did.

    Punished for being a woman,
    I put my head down—
    foggy memories
    are the only relics of sin
    in this untapped mental ghost town.

    They retrieve themselves
    without warning
    in a flash,
    and it is then that I feel
    my teeth start to gnash.

But as a woman,
I birth the resilience to know
our shared journeys of hitchhiking
will drive us to freedom
nine months from tomorrow.

    So many of my pages
    are filled in
    by co-authors
    whose silhouettes I can't find.
    So, is it plagiarism
    for me to speak
    if I believe it's all my fault
    in my mind?

Trust hushes me,
not to censor,
but to bring me to a standstill—
to give me a second to breathe
and halt scaling this hill.

I raise this truth to power,
a fruit juice glass to toast me—
sometimes, you don't get better;
you just learn to be.

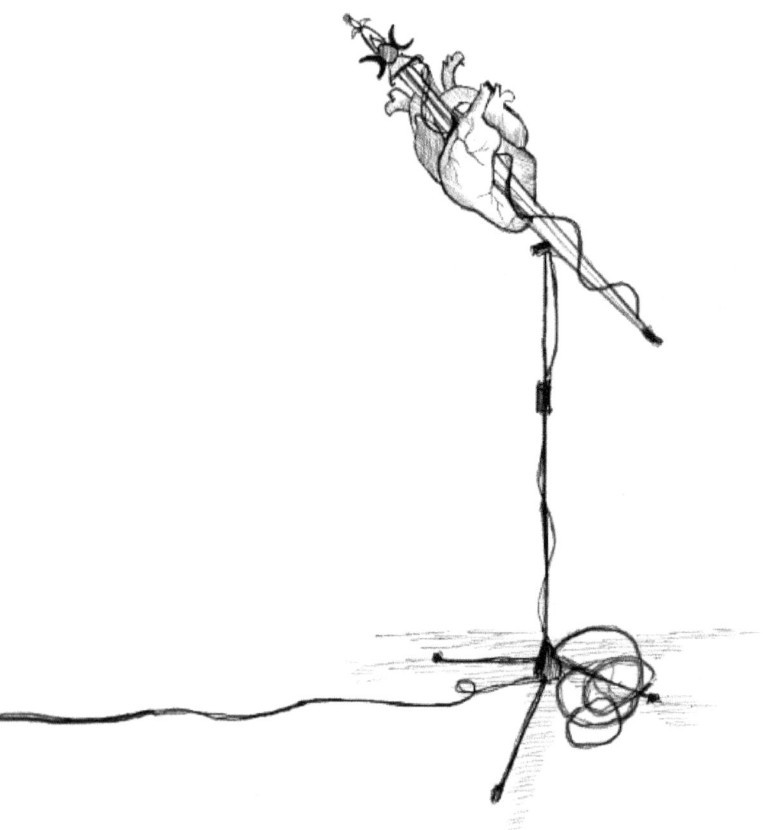

I Am Not a Poet

I am not a poet.
I am the whole damn poem.

The cacophony of symbols
recklessly strung together
in the middle of a sleepless night,
salvaging whatever is left of love
after yet another ferocious fight.

The uneven stanzas scribbled out
because they are not good enough
for you to fathom
as rhythmic,
as art,
as soothing to your heart.

The silences heard
when you reach the end,
sinking with your thoughts
of how to make amends.

I am the abrasive poem you write
by digging your fingernails
into my sandpaper flesh—
but this rugged tapestry,
sewn by your coarse tongue,
makes me want to start afresh.

So, I tear myself down,
piece by piece,
until my split soul
is discarded and tattered.

It waits for the spark
of your fiery passion
to ignite my skin—
now bruised and battered.

My very existence is the violent crime
of speaking out in a world
that renders me spineless—
then pats my back
and beams over my crib
to apologise for killing my kindness.

I wonder how to be a wordsmith
when I cannot create peace
out of the war waged on me—
it's easier to stay caged than break free.

But Poetry snatches my heart
right out of my beating chest
and gently places it on my sleeve
to wear on my violated honour's Eve.

A poet would have written bad poems
before they got to the good ones...
Am I a poet?

Blood runs thick,
but ink runs thicker—
my heated passion
is more than just a flicker.

My words turn heartbreak
into heart-wrenching music—
soulful lyrics that kindle fire
like logs in a kiln of brick.

With each stroke of my finger,
I trace my pattern of pessimism
and set my shackled heart free—
blank pages to you,
but poetry for me.

So, when I tell you,
I am not just a poet,
I am the whole damn poem,
I desire for your heart to desire
not my pale cover,
but my one-woman choir.

Let me serenade you to sleep
with lullabies that'll make you weep.

My knees scrape the carpet—
folded hands parallel to the tiles—
as I implore you not to shove me
at the back of your bookcase,
especially not with your signature,
sardonic little smile.

I beg you
not to let me lie
in the library
of my intrusive thoughts,
crumpling myself up,
writing,
furiously writing,

until the midnight oil
burns the poem in me alive,
until the poet in me
loses a thousand lives.

A poet would have concluded on the previous page...
But what do I know?
I am not a poet.

Chapter Two:

Of Love

and Healing

Poetry in Motion

You, my dear,
are the treasured masterpiece
on display in every gallery
of my beating heart.
For you, my dear,
are my favourite work of art.

Many visitors will glance,
as they stop by for tea.
If they stay by chance,
they will admire
what they perceive you to be.
Or perhaps, call you glitzy,
missing the underlying meaning
they cannot truly see.

Yet others will saunter
into different exhibits,
too bored and unfazed
to let you know
just how much
you deserve to be praised.

Unlike them,
I will patiently sit
on the wooden bench
that squarely faces
the rectangular wall you put up—
to let strangers see you,
but never let in,
to feel safety
only in your own skin.

But I want to wrap your frame
in my arms,
immersing you in the magic
of my cloak,
absorbing each flawless brush stroke
on your skin
into my own.

> Lead captures the depth of our conversations
> in the pages of my sketchbook,
> deconstructing the silent textures
> of your Art Noveau architecture.

If a picture speaks a thousand words,
then you are a charming poet,
and we are but lines—
not in the queues
outside this downtown studio,
but in the thick
of Shakespeare's First Folio.

Our story will be a classic—
remembered for centuries
after we are forgotten.

> My female gaze
> unwittingly memorises
> the colours in your eyes—
> a portrait of pure perfection
> as playful and enamouring
> as the charm in your fingers
> that strum along guitar strings.

You perform a little waltz
in the ballroom of my mind,
melding so beautifully
as an ancient Greek sculpture of the past,
and a dreamscape haze of my future.

You are poetry in motion,
and I vow to safekeep you
in my museum,
I do.

An Introvert's Guide
to Intimacy

True love will search for your face
in a crowded room,
then tiptoe to the balcony
where it knows you've stepped out;
damn you, social anxiety.

    It will offer you fruit juice,
    never badgering you to down beer,
    then set up two chairs and a table,
    and squeeze your hand to wordlessly convey,
    "We don't need to go back in.
    I promise I'm right here."

It will notice when you're weepy
and gently touch its sleeve to your cheek,
while you apologise for the makeup stain
that demands removal with bleach.

    True love will drive you back home
    because it knows about your past
    with taking cabs at twilight—
    hands delicately stacked on the gear,
    and eyes peripherally gazing
    at your dark aura
    it finds bright.

You'll tell it you prefer
bookstores and cafés,
where your chest won't tie knots,
or sober house parties
where the music is loud enough to dance,
yet faint enough to hear your thoughts.

A belly laugh will escape its mouth,
for it will find your quirks endearing.

True love will walk you
to your front door,
ring the bell,
and hug you goodbye,
but not before leaving you flushed—
an intimacy so loud,
in introverts,
it's hushed.

Stillness

My wallflower skin has settled into
the feeling of intimacy in quietness,
in the early hours
of the last of sleep—
a second to press pause,
a second for me to keep.

    Oh, to let go of tough love,
    and be gentle and kind to myself—
    basking in the yellow
    that warms my eyelids,
    and snuggles beside
    the plant on my bookshelf.

I lengthen my sore legs
until my toes reach
the edge of the bed,
then switch off the fan
and open the drapes
to watch the breeze and trees wed.

    My espresso machine whirs,
    ice cubes clinking cheers in my cup—
    brown and white and beige swirling
    to gently wake me up.

I make believe
the floor I lie on
is a boundless meadow of daisies,
where melodies drift by
on cotton candy clouds,
and words don't walk;
they fly.

Oh, to romanticise a love so fine,
soft and benign and all mine.
To have a heart that gives and receives,
and accepts that I'm the only one
who can connect with the innermost me.

And one morning,
I will sit in this field,
ambitiously ploughing through
until the mellow summer leaves
my winter daisies healed.

Nature narrates
how heat melts snow
in the storyline of her book,
inspiring me to find
serenity everywhere
if I just remember to look.

An Affirmation for Artists

Dear artist
(yes, I'm going to call you one),

    Here's to the summits
    at the heart of pain
    you have yet to conquer,
    and the helicopters
    roaring over scenic canyons
    you have yet to leap from.

Relish the adventure,
the spirit of discovery.

    Listen to the babbling brooks
    in the countryside
    of your imagination,
    noting down the notes
    for your fingers
    to strum on mandolins.

Slurp iced lattes loudly,
letting foam moustaches splutter,
and indulge in your own laughter
before wiping away your tune
on table cottons and fibres.

    Wildly wobble on seesaws
    and kick off from the earth
    into the boundless space
    you boldly tease—
    a limitless force
    in a universe of possibilities.

After all,
it took me 21 years
to find the confidence to speak.
So, even if you take longer,
or long to traverse in solitude,
I promise,
you will find what you seek.

Impostor Love

My love is a chrysalis
where sorrow and hope converge,
so my paper-cut wings
can fly me to a place
where paramours aren't purged.

    Here, impostors like me
    wear off-the-rack gowns
    fit for pretend weddings—
    declaring we'll get married,
    yet fearing mere flings.

I wish someone knew
how much it hurts
to be the poster child
for impostor converts.

I am a misfit
in a community of misfits
that has figured out
how to stand out.
But I don't belong,
so I shuffle my feet
to another table,
and silently sit down.

    Craving someone I haven't had
    is an experience rather queer—
    how can I feel
    both him and her
    as being so far,
    and still, so near?

My pondering is disrupted by music
as a couple graces the floor,
dancing a first dance
that'll outlive their last breath
by opening historical doors.

Even when the universe
aligned its stars
to misalign for our kind,
they bravely ignored
all the warning signs.

> You see,
> holding hands is a love language
> spoken by those who are free—
> the ones who play Cupid,
> while on a shooting spree.
>
> *They'll hardly hear our woes,*
> *and never legalise our vows.*

They'll say our unnatural strength
makes the Lord weaker—
an untrue tale, I believe,
but then again, I am not a seeker.

The sky angrily rumbles,
and shakes the land below—
a thousand bullets firing off
to put on a rainy show.

> Red, orange, yellow, green, blue, indigo, and violet.
> A kaleidoscope.
> *A prism.*

And then, it hit.
And everything starts to make sense
bit by bit.

My sponge eyes soak in
the colours of the rainbow,
and squeeze out tears
that finally let me see
where it starts,
and where it ends,
and how it all leads back to me.

I can don this straitjacket no more.
It's time to let my impostor love soar.

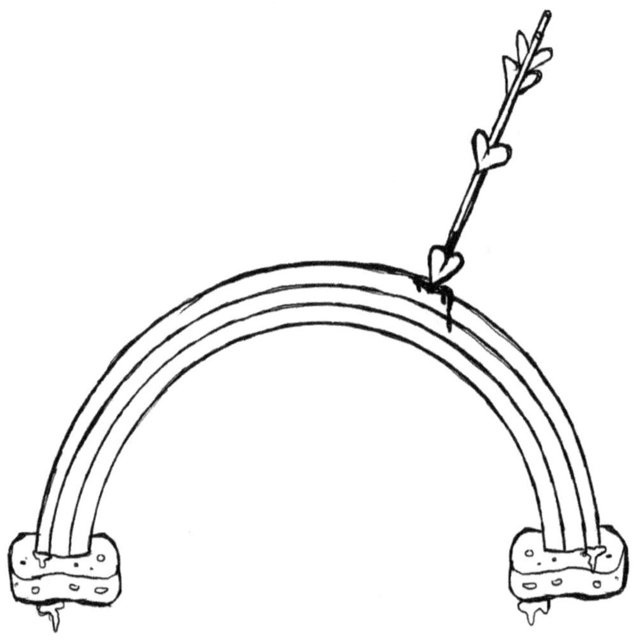

The Poem I Write
in My Dreams

I wish my voice sounded like
the poem I write in my dreams.

    My ballad strikes a balance
    between inspired and original,
    stopping readers in their tracks
    with hard-hitting messages so subliminal,
    they hop back onto my train
    to feel the thrill of travelling
    for the first time again.

    The commuters run their fingers
    along the metal seats
    where they first scraped
    my profound analogies—
    goosebumps roar
    in a hundred voices on their arms,
    going off like forgotten alarms.

My poem has a handcrafted selection
of free verses
about the illusion of luck;
they are capable of making someone
so sick to their stomach,
they're uncomfortable
in the big seat
their privilege bought
at the small table.

My poem bears an orderly structure
that reflects the structures
society orders us to sell,
except it's rife
with poignant politics
in fewer lines
than the ones leaders tell.

My lyrics are so moving,
they exalt whispers of wrath
that shape-shift
into megaphones to sing—
bringing about
revolutions and rebellions,
bringing down
dictators and kings.

But I'm too stranded on my own island
to brood about the world I left behind.

I am not a poet
is the only mantra
so discomforting,
it comforts me.

I recite it, over and over,
until I resort back to the cushioned box
I cannot think outside of,
to modulate my voice and sound like
the poem I write in my dreams.

Daily News
LONG LIVE

The Magic Within

A mahogany bookstore
and a basement library
close in proximity,
formed a galaxy
in my very own city.

> Their interstellar gas and dust
> collapsed within a molecular cloud,
> and after what felt like ages,
> a star was born from the shroud—
> *yellow flickering*
> *between yellowed pages.*

> In this star, I saw
> my childhood's saving grace—
> learning about magic and literature
> by hurtling straight through space.

You see, every Sunday,
my father read me grimoires
with spells so enchanting,
they let my festering wounds sing.

He presented me with the Vorpal Sword
and inspiration to ignite my soul,
as I slashed through the beasts in my mind—
hidden and hideous and dark as coal.

With the spirit of Achilles,
I spun straw into gold,
and befriended fiercely protective mongoose
in British bungalows.

Then, a fairy's friend whisked me away,
and I went with the flow
to a fantastical, timeless land
where kids don't grow.

> *I had my head up in the sky*
> *and built castles in the air there,*
> daydreaming about escaping reality,
> when all I really needed
> was unconditional care.

> And on nights that were safe,
> I curled up on my cot—
> "Tell me a tale about animal friends.
> 1...2...3...go!"
> And demanded a story on the spot.

His quicksilver tongue
glid over each word—
his imagination running
like a wild wolf
into untracked forests
of surrealism and sorcery,
defending its pack's
courage and curiosity.

My first royal minstrel
was a storyteller with a wide grin,
who conjured up an atmosphere
*for another to discover
the magic within.*

Rendezvous

If art imitates life,
there will soon be nothing left of you
but illegible tellings
from an untold memoir.

    As the world slips into a slumber,
    drawing its blinds,
    and losing sight of its horizon
    over the obsidian sea,
    specks of yearning take over
    the little that it spared of me.

If I never see you again,
will you promise to store
merry episodic memories
of one last rendezvous with me?

Shall we go apple picking,
or for a paddleboat ride
in the Italian countryside?
Or maybe curl up in the woods—
just us in a secluded cabin—
and unravel the magic within?

    But the clock started ticking
    much earlier than I thought,
    and didn't stop for two years
    when you hid away and didn't reappear.

    But our chronicle continued—
    Running.
    Regretting.
    Reconciling.

Every hardship
that got lost in translation,
finally finds meaning
in our resurfaced scheming.

> You remember how to listen
> and take my sorrow as your own,
> *creating an Aurora Borealis*
> *out of the monochrome.*

Oh, Poetry,
my childhood sweetheart,
I pray you never let me
let you go again.

This illustration was originally designed as a tattoo for the author
by Harsh Makwana, a tattoo artist at Alva (Al's) Tattoo Studio,
Mumbai.

Balcony Plant

Someday,
someone will come along
and cherish me to their core.
They'll follow along the perforated line
of my makeshift cardboard planter,
and give me room
to grow even more.

    I will be an enormous plant
    peeking through window grills,
    excitedly waving my leaves
    to plants in other balconies.

I will not shrink down
to an indoor bonsai—
pruned and well-sized,
but lonely and browned.

    I wish that for you too.
    For you to heal
    and absorb nutrition
    from soil that's not too much—
    that doesn't make you squirm
    with an ephemeral touch.

I do
want us to thrive—
just in different balconies
this time.

Little Whimsies

Journalling once prompted me to ponder,
"When do I feel most in tune with myself?"

I am a poet, I thought.
There could be headlights
illuminating a deep meaning
somewhere in my brain's parking lot.

    But all I found was a vintage car
    drawn by a charioteer with leather straps on,
    in the age of typewriters and vinyl players—
    polaroid snapshots of an era bygone.

    I adamantly took my place
    at the window seat
    just like I do on planes and trains,
    and anywhere with movement, really—
    a bird's-eye view
    of the bokeh and the blurred,
    intentionally seeing nothing clearly.

I envisioned myself sitting tight for the ride,
and pulled out a half-read Sylvia Plath book
with highlights and annotations
in the aftermath of my first look.

The radio recreated my favourite album,
one that was years ahead of its time—
music to my ears like fantasy folklore,
with wistful and bittersweet rhymes.

The clock struck twelve,
and I silently placed
someone, somewhere in the world,
whispering, *"Happy birthday."*

I reminisced about the year
no one remembered mine,
or at least as far as I could tell.
But there was still a spark in my heart—
perhaps a stranger had wished me well.

I opened my journal
to the next blank page.

I am not a poet, I wrote.
I feel most in tune with myself,
not through flowery metaphors in grasslands,
or revolutionary battles with words,
but through the eccentric routines
that make me, me—
these little whimsies.

Ladies Compartment

First published in *Rara Avis 2023*—the poetry anthology by the Department of Literary Arts, Extra Curricular Committee, St. Xavier's College, Mumbai.

Ladies Compartment is an artistic escape from the ordinary; concurrently, it is rooted in the idea that art lives in the ordinary. I believe in the power of the Divine Feminine—even among strangers. This piece celebrates the underrated moments that have transformed my train journeys into a treasure chest of cherished memories. I'd like to invite you to view some photographs I've captured of the Mumbai Local through a feminist lens.

A lifeline that wraps itself
as a front porch
around the city
celebrated for housing dreams,
bringing vibrancy to
hellos and goodbyes,
weaving stories from
children's laughs and sellers' outcries—
Mumbai, *meri jaan,* ki *jaan*[1]—
Mumbai Local.

    Where the fragrance of crushed mogras
    wafts through the ladies compartment,
    and settles on the 20-rupee-*jhumkas*[2]
    I should've impulsively bought, but I didn't.

1   Translation: The life of Mumbai, my life.
2   Traditional Indian earrings, which are typically bell-shaped.

Where poems write themselves
in the space between
the vada and the pav,
and shiver under shared umbrellas
on the days we collectively sigh,
"Baarish, chale jao![3]*"*

> Where pieces of different love languages
> curl up into the mosaic
> of one mother tongue
> to sing songs previously unsung
> at Bandra, *Baandra,* and *Vaandre.*

Where loneliness meets humanity,
immersing its Parle-G in cutting chai,
bonding over tote bags with Bollywood lyrics,
and relishing the concrete jungle safari ride.

> Where this little world of women
> is a railway platform of co-existence—
> of yellowed money stowed
> in padded blouses
> and glittery phone covers,
> of house keys clanking
> on saree-clad waists
> and between the interlaced fingers
> of forbidden lovers.

Where, when a woman stands close to me,
anxiously glancing at a man left lurking behind,
she finds solace in my Divine Feminine brushstrokes—
an unpainted masterpiece
by Mumbai's local womankind.

3   Translation: Rain, go away!

The Miracle of Wonderland

First published in *Tartan 2017*—the annual magazine of
Bombay Scottish School, Mahim, Mumbai.

I sat down on the soft grass,
fresh and green,
and opened my favourite book to read.

Suddenly, by me flew
a beautiful butterfly,
looking proud and keen
to show me her wings of jade,
spotted with crimson too.

I stopped reading the book
and placed it on the ground,
as my eyes cherished another story
unfurled all around.

    Never before had I seen pink flowers
    blooming before my eyes,
    or baby caterpillars
    wrapped in white, silk cocoons,
    ready to say their goodbyes.

Bright yellow sparrows
chirped melodiously
high up on the treetops,
and a cunning black spider
weaving his web,
dangling from a strand, dropped.

In a murky puddle,
dark green frogs
hopped and splashed about
to rejoice in the news
of the leaving drought.

    A brown bear slowly peered
    from behind the bushes,
    and a woodpecker's strong beak
    on the bark, still pushes.

A whizzing, striped bee
sat on a flower
and sipped nectar,
and an aura of joy
spread around this hectare.

    Then night fell on the forest
    like a purple blanket.

    Colonies of jet-black bats
    filled the night sky,
    and from a slowly-cracking egg
    came a piercing cry.

    The chatter was replaced
    by a hush of silence
    to signal the end
    of the forest's day,
    and from that moment,
    incredible Wonderland,
    for you,
    I have no words left to say.

Nomad

Love is a nomad
without a permanent address—
a free spirit reading Rumi
to uncover more with less.

> She wanders beyond the confines
> of laws, norms, and contracts
> to park her luminous caravan
> on the footpath of whoever attracts.

> Jiving with strangers
> on uneven pavements
> in glossy high heels,
> and on hardwood kitchen floors
> in worn-out fuzzy socks,
> *she lets herself feel all the feels.*

Love nestles in the crevices,
waiting for me to seek.

The song I can't help but hum.
The friend who checks in when I keep mum.
The stuffed bear I cuddle to sleep.
The healthy snack my mother makes me keep.
The movie on my autoplay.
Other shy girls with so much to say.

> My heart is a cornucopia of emotions—
> tangerines overflowing in baskets
> at the local farmer's market.

Yet, my heart is just as heavy
as the damp soil that grew those fruits—
decaying from the tip to the roots.

> *Love slips through the cracks,*
> *challenging me to seek.*

> The concert I can't attend because my ears throb.
> The friend who moved away for a new job.
> The comfort toy that frayed enough to toss out.
> The apple that rotted and made my mother pout.
> The movie that's full of gore.
> *Most shy girls with no one to listen to their lore.*

I cry now,
but soon, I'll be glad,
for Love doesn't settle down;
she liberally roams around.

This nomad is a feather in the breeze—
forever billowing, never at ease.

> Love will leave to return
> in a different hobby
> and a different companion—
> *when the time is right*
> *to hold on tight.*

Outgrowing My Childhood Best Friend

Anger has been by my side,
come what may.
I feel him at a primal level,
aggressively moulding me like clay.

He comes to me as a reflex,
pampering me with a siren's call,
and protecting me from the slides
that once made me slip and fall.

I want to shush his voice,
even when it sounds like greyed wisdom,
and have this innate monarch
rule a different kingdom.

But Anger tacitly pushes people away
even when he is a mute king
to finally get me my turn
on the playground swing.

It must have been child's play for him,
I thought,
as I watched how, for me,
someone fought.

Anger arises and unfolds
his hidden strength
for all to see.
But no one ever told him
that being bullied
often makes you a bully.

Anger packs a punch
to flaunt his power,
overcompensating for all the times
he shamefully let his head cower.

I know exactly which buttons he pushes.
I know exactly which buttons he makes me push.

    He is not remorseful,
    despite being guilty.
    Anger does not apologise,
    or let Resilience heal me.

    Is there space
    for different voices to be heard,
    without being steamrolled
    by my companion's foul words?

Love organically blossoms
between childhood best friends,
but not all friendships are healthy
or genuinely aim to mend.

    I'm beginning to decipher
    Anger's façade
    of trickery and lies,
    and embracing Resilience,
    my newfound ally,
    by cutting off all juvenile ties.

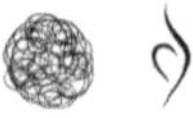

Depression Room

Everything my depression
skims through
solidifies to nothing.

Eyes full of life
turn as cold as the stone
of the countryside English cottage
I wish to someday own.

I would call it the Midas touch,
but gold is a colour too rich
for my palette to fathom.

It's all too loud,
it's all too much.

My room is my sanctuary—
a place for the wilderness
to exist untamed and free,
or at least that was my goal.

Perfectly systematic and stacked,
my room is a fallacy—
everything is under control.

I like my pastel stationery
in desk organisers,
and my uncreased clothes
on wooden hangers,
but oh, Depression is a despiser.

She cuts deep,
marking her territory
with red-blue blood
on my flaky skin.
"Welcome to *my* room", Depression says,
holding my face by the chin.

    My stationery is strewn
    under a mound of clothes,
    creating a mess chaotic enough
    to turn a control freak
    into a complete wreck.
    Suddenly, I see a mountain—
    the only terrain I'd hate to trek.

I turn to my inviting bed—
now a dwelling for Insomnia.
She takes my place on the right side
and drinks coffee in my pyjamas.

Misery loves company,
or does she?

    She throws ragged towels over my mirror
    so I don't accidentally see how
    I'll eat enough to feed a country,
    or starve like most people there now.
    Which hyperbole will my body dysmorphia pick today?

I search for shelter in someone else,
believing they can pull me out,
but I'm too far down this rabbit hole
for even them to hear me shout.

Toxic and *manipulative*
are echoes shoved down the dirt,
but all I ever wanted
was to be wanted,
with neither of us
discoloured or hurt.

> The floor sympathises with me
> and pats itself down to say,
> "I'm a place that creates space.
> On me, you can comfortably lay."

> I recall each time I sat motionless,
> unbathed in dried sweat for days,
> hopelessly wanting them by my side
> as I cried and cried and cried.

No one is coming to save me
or help me clean my depression room.
The only cape a superhero can drape
is me with a bucket and broom.

I start in small piles,
rigorously mopping up Doubt,
using headphones to block out the psyche
that tries to psych me out.

> Perfectly systematic and stacked,
> my room is a reality—
> *everything is under control.*

Shoebox Memories

4:00 am on a Wednesday,
cross-legged, eyes puffy,
I hold onto the last
of people who left
in shoebox memories,
now so stuffy.

> In the distance, there's a mirage
> of remembrances with no regrets—
> foreshadowing the thirst
> this cache could not quench.

> *The temperature riots,*
> *and my time capsule quiets.*

Tokens from a beau
with whom I chewed honeycomb,
tasting nectar in his gentle gestures—
Unerased first love that felt like home.

Clandestine confessions
and strawberry yoghurt,
grandparents' rings
and little black skirts—
a past soulmate
I still hold in high regard,
but it's my turn to play
and I'm charring his Joker card.

Expired tickets from metro rides
I no longer take to meet him.
Candles from the church we visited
on a Sunday morning whim.

    Restaurant bills,
    heart-printed straws,
    and Christmas cards
    from the girl I wished would stay,
    and transcend from being my best friend
    to my bridesmaid one day.

I placed my hands
right into the eyewall
of this handmade tornado,
letting my eyes meet those of the storm,
deriving calm from conceivable harm.

Grey incense swirled under my feet,
my religion rebirthed as I swore
to seek atonement
for setting this bonfire
that finally let all of you go.

    I burned what we had into the ground,
    and saw myself emerge,
    seared from the ashes around—
    a phoenix who cried healing tears
    onto the last seven years.

And, just like that,
all of you evanesced,
smudging my hands with soot—
but this time, I'm the one
who masterminded your escape route.

Notice Me

I don't want you
to love me,
respect me,
or even care about me.

But I need you
to notice me.

    I need you to notice
    how your nostrils flare up
    and your chest swells with indignation
    at the thought of my thoughts
    raising blizzards and snowstorms.

    Hurricanes are named after people for a reason...
    right?

Sometimes, the cloud of life
has no silver lining—
just a black one
that precipitates
onto the pages of journals
before it's too late.

    I am not the orchard of optimism,
    where flower beds harbour
    plenty of positivity,
    or the girl who always prays
    for lessons in losses,
    and trusts that everything will be okay.

I am a testament to reality
that hits you
like an epiphany.

    No, I don't pretend
    the world is a beautiful place
    of unconditional love
    and endless choices,
    where the destination is peripheral—
    a fence of the perpetual chase.

I see things differently,
which could change how you view me.

    I think you'll steer your car away
    toward the warm embrace
    of the longest day,
    and soak up light
    from the summer solstice
    to make your world a little less grey.

    Or maybe you'll find
    an emerging infatuation
    with my solar eclipse,
    and how my lunar maria smiles
    are powerful enough
    to block even the sun,
    even if only for a little while.

Whichever route you choose,
I hope you choose to notice me.

I hope you choose me.

Heirloom

Violence has been passed down to me
like an unwanted heirloom.

It orders me
to ignore my own needs,
coddle the treasure,
and nurture it
until it fills me up
and makes me bleed.

　　To care is to spout cruelty—
　　the kind that withholds kindness.

　　Love is a bruised kiss
　　that slices through
　　the shoulder blades
　　of the next of kin—
　　sharp as a knife,
　　barely twisted in.

*But you make me pull the dagger out
to admire the shades of burgundy.*

You see,
abuse is a muse,
looming over a blank canvas
in crimson splatters of paint,
and just a tinge of red-blue hues.

And I?
I am doe-eyed as I watch
the religious artwork
of a devotee who worships booze.

> *Fearful screams behind broken doors,*
> *crates of bottles on the living room floor.*

> Or at least that is the narrative
> I was advised never to give—
> just like those before me
> who wore the same muzzle,
> gaslighting themselves
> in order to live.

I was too young
to grow up that fast.

And as I did,
trauma thinned my hair—
I couldn't romanticise the pain
that had only damaged me
beyond repair.

> But don't we get hurt
> by those who care?
> Doesn't that which bewitches,
> throw you against the wall—
> a herb in a concoction,
> poisoned to make you fall?

Abuse is not anyone's muse.
But little girls don't know any better.
The little girl in me didn't know any better.

So, she loved through the pain,
confusing the two,
raising herself,
and learning to survive
by being angry and shrew.

Violence ran through her veins,
hostile and wanting an outlet
to turn all that she had seen
into art—
a tinge of red-blue hues
on the canvas of her own flesh,
as she struggled to start afresh.

It takes everything in me
to unconditionally love
this disobedient inner child,
and lead by example,
so she can forgive herself
through a love that is gentle and mild.

I have toiled for years on end
to blend amethyst and fairy dust
into a stunning pendant—
a sparkle of joy draped around her neck,
with a clasp of trust that won't rust.

She will lazily toss
her feet over the couch,
swinging them to and fro,
giggling at age-old bedtime stories,
and knowing when to say no.

She will forge a fresh legacy
filled with squeals
and devoid of screams.

Purple hope will course through
my future daughter's veins,
and I will smile at her,
having known all along—
*to build love from scratch
is never in vain.*

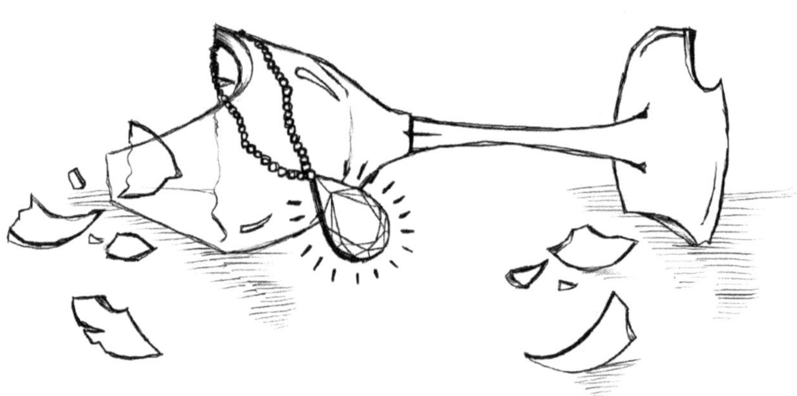

Reparenting

When it comes to mental health,
the only real difference
between my parents and me
is resources and vocabulary.

They support my pursuit of Psychology,
but hesitate to try therapy,
representing generations of minds
forbidden from being free.

> We talk of reparenting
> our adult selves,
> affirming our need
> for safety and stability—
> but what about all the inner children
> we don't bother to see?

As I tread through tangled wires,
tripping over the chaos
that sheathes me like a second skin,
I think about how naturally
most parents wear theirs.

About how pride stops them from admitting
they, too, deserved emotional care.

> *Do you know the destruction it takes*
> *to break cycles ever so slowly?*
> *The courage you have to muster*
> *to unravel symptom clusters?*

The absent adults in our lives,
required present ones in theirs—
for the emotional landscape
where we fail to find joy,
is where they grew up
with just enough food
and not enough toys.

Their parents
and their parents' parents
had the same scant knowledge,
which makes us see
the cause of the cycle
at the start of the family tree.

The roots are long and thick;
it is a well-guarded dungeon, indeed.
But I know the mystical phrase
that'll meet the dragon's needs.

I have finally made a breakthrough,
and taken what was mine
from the start—
*glowing embers of healing
in the chambers of my heart.*

And I have something for you, too.

Here's a plain white slate
to write your new story—
acknowledge the gory past,
but hope for future glory.

One Christmas Eve

First published in *Tartan 2012*—the annual magazine of Bombay Scottish School, Mahim, Mumbai.

Looking back on this piece fills my heart with warmth and nostalgia. It feels right to place my first published poem as the last one because it captures how my journey has come full circle. I can't help but imagine my nine-year-old self, who penned *One Christmas Eve,* smiling at how poetry is *still there* for her 21-year-old self. I want to take this moment to remind her that we were, and always will be, a poet.

Today is the night of Christmas Eve,
and a magical feeling makes me believe
that everything nice will happen to me—
oh, I just can't wait to see!

    What will be filled in my stockings?
    Video games, books, and of course,
    lots of candy!
    As I dream about yummy treats,
    Santa comes to my door knocking.

    He takes me to the icy North Pole
    on a sledge ride.
    Wow! Utterly rocking!

At the North Pole,
I can see the elves,
the reindeer,
and some light-coloured mansion.

Santa's workshop, could it be?
Behind these extraordinary, shimmering
Northern Lights that I see!

"Look at the lovely gifts in your stockings!"
My mother wakes me up with exhilaration.

But what about the workshop?
The Aurora lights?
The sledge rides?

A dream it was,
the loveliest I've had—
or could it be that Santa
was my very own dad?

Chapter Three:

Of Letters

and Musings

Between the Lines

Have you noticed that we read lines, but rarely between them? We don't pause to question why a stanza is on the subsequent page, or why the poet chose to use a semicolon instead of a comma. However, poetry encompasses so much more than figurative language, rhythmic expressions, and vivid imagery.

Poetry is also about the gaps that fill silences.

You see, appreciating poetry involves decrypting the subtler nuances we often disregard as 'poetic', much like:

The interlude that builds suspense
before the bridge
in a new pop song.

The silver that melts
into homemade chocolate cake
before it turns brown.

How my nose can taste the rain
because it breathes in petrichor
before it hears the drizzle.

On some days, I open my heart like a gigantic gate that slowly swings to let everyone in and out. On other days, I triple-lock it and throw the key so high up in the sky that it lands on a passing plane, never to be seen again.

But when I wrote my first letter to this ornate gate, it skipped beats before I even sealed the flap.

My heart found its lifeline in words before my eyes could read them.

My ideas took human form before my hands could form a skeleton out of them.

When I read a book for the first time, I only focused on the black text and found myself being invited to someone else's gate. There, I saw fear, confidence, accomplishment, elation, guilt, and all the in-betweens they let enter. But amid the hubbub, the silence became deafening, and my sensitive ears missed the point— the pinpoint location on the map that could only be reached through unsaid expressions between the lines.

And so, I began to acknowledge the white space as much as the black text.

I found the freedom to catch my breath and savour one moment before transitioning to the next. I assigned a new significance to this moment by reflecting on my own fear, confidence, accomplishment, elation, guilt, and all the other in-betweens I let enter.

When my reveries take over the city, they leave my gates wide open and write personalised letters to everything and everyone: feelings, disorders, people, and even themselves.

There is magic in interweaving poetry into prose, prose into poetry, and both of them into letters. *Will you read between the lines of my letters?*

Surviving Suicide

I live in a country where mental health infrastructure is virtually non-existent. Here, cultural taboos are deeply ingrained in institutions such as workplaces and family systems. Young adults are discouraged from expressing 'morbid' and 'gruesome' thoughts, and if we do, these thoughts are trivialised, dismissed as attention-seeking, or subjected to relentless mockery.

> Enduring pain in secrecy, only to have it discovered when it is unfortunately too late, appears to be our sole escape.

As banal as it may sound, I want to reiterate the message that *it is okay not to be okay*. I am tired of pretending that I am fine, and of others doing the same. I cannot exclusively love happy-go-lucky people who wear a smile as if it's sewn onto their faces. Instead, I want to vocalise that my mental battles have the potential to escalate into full-blown wars. I believe that my catastrophising is just as human as others' optimism.

> In this journal entry, I attempt to seek control over the narrative of an incident that, ironically enough, turned my life around.

I'm still petrified to process the events that took place on 15th March 2023, let alone summon the courage to share my story. Nevertheless, I acknowledge that what I went through was real and traumatising. It wasn't a 'gastrointestinal infection', as disseminated to everyone; it was an intentional suicide attempt. *And I failed. Miserably. Again.*

It wasn't my first time trying to die, but it was my first time suffering it like never before.

Being hospitalised for more than a day, just days after turning 21, is no joke. Having tubes painfully thrust down your nostrils to pump out your stomach, is no laughing matter. A needle-like sensation piercing through your throat for 8 hours—to the extent that you need to type on your phone to communicate, and avoid drinking water even through a bottle cap—is not humorous. How about lying helpless in a casualty room while a nurse performs an ECG, draws pints of blood, and subjects you to five different tests? Or needing an IV drip to supply you with nutrients because your depression cruelly refused to let you eat in the last two days? Correct. Not amusing.

Strangely, the staff at the first hospital my sister rushed me to, and the authorities who took my statement at the second one, seemed to find my case funny. It was one to be sensationalised for months to come. When I wasn't laughed at, I was admonished.

"Why do you young people do wrong things like this?"
"Don't do this next time because it stresses out the people around you."
"Don't invite yourself to the hospital when you don't have a real problem."

How many times does someone have to come bawling for help, only to be shut out by the very people who are supposed to help?

How many hushed deaths will it take for us
to care about the silent killer?

How many questions do I have to ask to get answers?

I lost myself the night I relived every horrific thing that had happened in my 21 years of existence. I didn't want to live anymore; I had already hurt too much. My body involuntarily curled up in a corner of my bedroom, pleading with me to crawl out of my skin and let my soul seek peace. At that moment, I recalled Vincent van Gogh's apparent last words before he took his own life—*"The sadness will last forever."*

Van Gogh used extensive amounts of yellow in his artwork. It is believed that he even ingested yellow paint to "get the happiness inside him". So, I decided to eat my own yellow paint and try, for one last time, to get the happiness inside me too.

There is so much stigma around the word 'suicide' that I almost didn't include the theme in the book that is closest to my heart—my own. I was scared to be vulnerable and highlight the raw truth of my own neurosis. How would my friends, acquaintances, and strangers alike perceive me? What would they say about my actions, my selfishness, my potential, my family, my seemingly 'normal' life, and the privileges that come with it? The list of questions is endless, especially in a society where survivors are made to feel like suicide is a *choice*.

The longer we place our fingers to our mouths,
the more we're going to use them to pull the
trigger.

The more we pretend that it isn't happening
to someone we know, the more they are at
risk of ending up in the hospital.

And they might not be as fortunate as I was. Their family members might not drop everything to be by their side. Their sisters, brother-in-law, father, uncle, and aunt might not remain with them, holding their hands through the entire traumatic process. Their mother might not fly in from a distant city upon hearing the news, only to stay with them overnight. Their best friends might not visit their hospital room with handwritten notes, photographs, and flowers (that were unfortunately confiscated). They might not get the *enormous* amount of support and love that I am still so grateful to have received.

We need to stop shoving the problem at the back
of a drawer like a secret cutting knife. Trust me,
I know.

This letter is dedicated to anyone who has faced a loss—whether it's a hobby, a lover, a pet, or a family member. It could even be missing out on the last day of college when your friends took graduation pictures and signed each other's shirts because you were in suicide recovery. Each kind of loss leaves a different void—an amoeba-shaped emptiness that seems impossible to fill perfectly.

And yet, I want you to remember that a semicolon stands for a sentence that an author *could have ended but chose to continue.*

In January 2022, I got a semicolon tattooed on my left wrist to symbolise my solidarity with suicide prevention and other mental health issues. I hope this story serves as a similar reminder for you. Your sentence, and consequently your story, is a work in progress. You can still experience beautiful chapters, even if it means enduring the ones smeared in turmoil first.

I see you and I hear you; it is not as simple as motivational speakers brimming over with toxic positivity make it out to be.

So, we will grieve together, and we will hope to heal together.

We will persist to exist.

Sometimes, that is more than enough.

Always, *you* are more than enough.

28th December 2022

New Beginnings

Each year brings with it the promise of revival.

It is a well-thumbed page waiting to be turned.

It is found somewhere atop a turret room on a mountain.

It is a water lily on the brink of blooming in this minuscule garden we call life.

A new year is defined by many metaphors. Today, I am mulling over the last one, as I sit by a lily pad like a frog with a lifetime of hopping and skipping about left in her.

I have been a writer all my life, but I have only recently come to terms with the fact that love is...boundless. Love is not a jukebox that plays my favourite songs when I fill it up with golden coins of affection. Love cannot be captured within the loops of my cursive letters or the warmth of my partner's interlaced fingers.

Love is beautiful in its own right—a montage of forgotten sprigs in jean pockets and yellowed polaroids in phone covers. Love holds up a mirror to the bottomless pit of my fears and softly whispers, *"You will be okay as long as I live here."*

This year, I chose to love through all the butterfly wings my little heart could flutter with.

I evolved into a platonic lover when I, quite literally, climbed mountains and braved thunderstorms with my chosen family. I became a hopeless romantic when I painted the sky hues of lavender, and my muse held my paint-stained hands, affirming that purple was his new favourite colour.

Finally, I discovered love in the depths of my bandaged wounds. I kissed my childhood scars and promised them we would heal together. That we would chart a new map, and with it, a new road to our destiny. We have accepted the unforgiving past, and are now taking baby steps towards the unknown future.

The coming year will only bring more love, as it stands on the welcome mat of my front door, with my foster cat, Coco, sitting patiently at its feet.

So, here's to the poems yet to ignite a fire in the furnace of my mind, and the songs yet to spin yarns of melodies in my soul. *I will embrace you with love, love, and lots of love.*

Solo Date

I have had three relationships in the last four years, each of which holds significance for me due to different reasons. However, I spent little time being single between them.

My craving for romantic love stems from a place of co-dependence in relationships. I believe that if I love someone with my entire heart and soul, my inherent loneliness will fade into oblivion.

Recently, I had an epiphany that this pattern of obsessively prioritising another's needs over my own, is destructive for both of us. It makes me clingy and compels them to repeatedly reassure me that I am, in fact, their significant other.

However, being merged with my *other half* conveys that I am *only half* a person. This incomplete version of myself struggles to establish a stable sense of self. She fails to appreciate the value of becoming whole.

I want to consciously rewrite this narrative. I am determined to love myself with both halves of my own whole.

A past lover once advised me to keep all the love that I had for him, for myself. *And today, I will.*

5th May 2023

2:05 p.m.
I'm half-asleep as I instinctively reach for a cottagecore sundress from my cupboard—honey-yellow adorned with crimson flowers. It features a Carmen neckline and a smocked top that cinches at my waist before flaring out. I particularly adore the tassels that gracefully dangle from the ends of both sleeves.

I think I'll wear a yellow hairband to complete my look. A close friend gifted it to me on my birthday. I have a reputation for frequently wearing hairbands.

I wonder if he remembers how I always colour-coordinate them with my outfits.

2:10 p.m.
I'm standing close to the mirror, carefully applying *kohl*[1] to underline my moist waterline. This morning, I woke up from a dream where he called me outside his prom venue because he had something important to share. He had moved on and wanted me to hear about it from him first. His girlfriend was intelligent, beautiful, and charming, of course. I watched him dance with her the way I wanted him to with me. He was the happiest I'd ever seen him. I smiled sadly as he booked me a cab to drop me back home.

But my home stood in front of me, *building new foundations and painting over faded mauve-blue walls with different colours.* I wished him a happy life, but a little part of me wished it were with me instead.

---

1   This refers to the black powder that is often used in eye makeup, especially in Eastern countries. It is also called *kajal*.

2:17 p.m.

It turns out I spent 7 minutes reliving that dream. I'm going to shrug off my thoughts and pull black liquid across my left eyelid in one go. After that, I think I'll use the blush that my sister's fiancé gifted her on her birthday. She had graciously kept it on my table, along with a handwritten note saying that it would suit my skin tone better. I'm lightly tapping it in circular motions, blending it from my cheekbones up to my temples.

I wonder if he remembers watching me apply blush in my mirror, just like this.

2:40 p.m.

I haven't typed in a while because I was figuring out my mode of transportation. I had planned to hail an autorickshaw outside my building. While one driver was contemplating whether or not to take me, another one stopped and gestured that I could get in. I asked him if he would go to Pali Village, and he said he'd have me there in no time.

I wonder if he contemplates stopping by when he crosses my lane.

3:02 p.m.

A few minutes ago, the driver got a call; something had come up. He informed me that he could not take me to Pali Village. Then, he called his friend, who was nearby and had agreed to give me a ride. I found the whole interaction quite thoughtful.

Now, I'm opening my brown bag to take out a book by Mahmoud Darwish; I want to understand what it's truly like to be *In the Presence of Absence*. I'm also pulling out my earphones with my right hand as I type this with my left hand. I want to read for a bit and let the shaky letters imprint themselves on me.

But my mind keeps wandering back to how, when I was getting ready, I thought a brown bag on a yellow dress would make me feel like a human sunflower. And it does. I wore a black skirt with sunflowers printed on it, this day last year.

I wonder if he thinks of me when he sees sunflowers.

4:03 p.m.
I'm on my way back home now because I have a therapy session at 5:00 p.m. I had planned to leave by 4:30 p.m. to account for the time spent buying sunflowers, but I couldn't spot my favourite roadside flower stall today. There was just a grey space where there are usually pinks, reds, and greens. But I wasn't upset about it. After all, I had just stepped out of my shell and experienced independence in a way that was incredibly fulfilling and healing.

Let me take you through my solo date!

I strolled through a lane with colourful cottages and dense trees lining the street—a rare sight in my hometown. Then, I was enthralled by a solo exhibition at an art gallery called Art and Charlie.

Saviya Lopes, the artist, spoke a visual language of immigration, matriarchy, and empowerment. Of the agency of the female body. Of intelligence being stored in hands that carry out physical and emotional labour.

These women's hands—each labelled with their rightful names—told stories of tradition. Of generations of women's hands measuring ingredients, calculating time, and weaving magic out of stitches. Of feminists who were so ahead of their time, they were feminists before they even knew the term.

I also made friends with someone at the gallery. As I sat with her, in that sanctuary of sisterhood, I felt love dissolve into my skin—*oh, how I loved being a woman.*

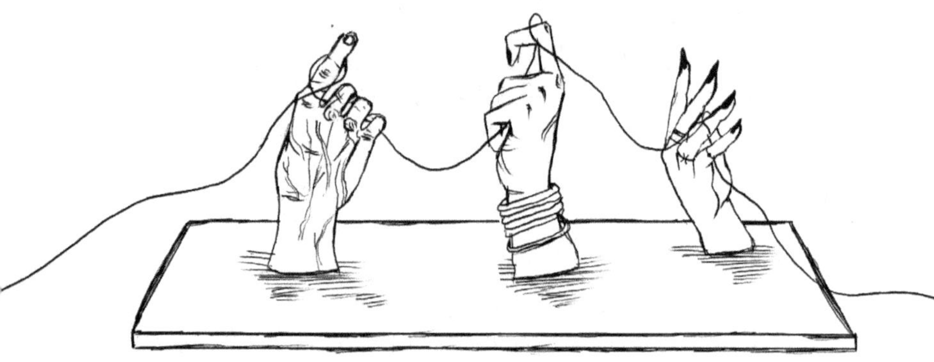

6th May 2023

6:32 a.m.
My therapist cancelled our session yesterday, which was actually a relief; I was not in the mood to unpack anything. I hadn't met my closest friends in a while, so I invited them over for dinner. One of them stayed the night and shared personal stories from her childhood with me. I felt deep empathy for her. Knowing what she went through made me want to wrap her in the duvet and reassure her that she's safe now. She already knows how proud I am of her, *but strong people need to hear it out loud too.*

I'm accustomed to staying up until sunrise because I enjoy writing through the night. I've written most of this book during the night. However, my friend was exhausted after a long day at work, so she went to sleep. Now, I'm lying in bed, squinting at my Notes app in the pitch dark because I can't remember where I left my glasses.

For now, let's return to my solo date and my unlikely friend. The last thing I expected was to bond with a stranger over fashion and heartbreak, but that's exactly what happened. She told me how she used heartbreak as an inspiration to start writing again, and I laughed because I was doing the same thing. We exchanged numbers, promised to meet at another exhibition again, and parted ways.

There was a tiny, overpriced coffee shop just below the gallery. I ordered an iced oat milk latte, adjusted my earphones, and wrapped my comfort song around me like a cardigan. After collecting my coffee, I started walking towards my favourite roadside flower shop (which, at the time, I didn't know was closed).

Suddenly, I spotted hints of orange, brown, and white—a cat. It was sunbathing on the stairs of its owner's house and affectionately meowed when I beamed at it. I bent down to pet its soft head but promptly ran away when I heard footsteps approaching from inside.

I apologise for these journal entries being a mess. Initially, I wanted to document each happening as it came. But once I was in the art gallery, I became part of the muslin and handwritten scrapbooks and forgot to type live updates.

I didn't even think about him. Until now.

I finally kept all the love that I had for him, for myself.

Piscean Moons

I am a Piscean impressionist,
immersed in the tranquillity
of the crystal water,
where white lilies float
like unmelting paper boats.

Two copper fish swirl around,
nibbling at my dipped toes,
while I watch the ripples
in the moonlight's gleam,
glisten like pearls in a silvery dream.

I first fell in love with the universe when I visited Nehru Planetarium as a wide-eyed child. I marvelled at the trails left behind by the planets dancing across the ceiling. I soaked in the vastness of the Milky Way. I felt connected to something bigger than myself. *Even the dome-shaped starry sky couldn't contain my desire to charm my new muse.*

Years later, the mystique surrounding the Creation still held me spellbound. The idea that magical forces eternally aligned themselves to interlace the ethereal and the real, captivated me. I started believing that if I was part of this universe, the extraordinary lived and grew within me too. And it started from the very day I was born.

3/3 has always been a special stitch in the fabric of my cosmic journey. As I was about to turn the 21st yarn over my needles, I wanted to sew a new element into my patchwork quilt—a medley of three celestial bodies.

This birthday, I wanted to embody the process of becoming and unbecoming with my guardian angel— the moon. She floats above me every day, lulling me to sleep by strumming songs on her ukulele and scribbling sonnets in her journal. A fellow Piscean spirit, she is adventurous, dreamy, and poetic.

She inspired me to redefine our zodiac sign— two fish swimming in opposite directions, bound by a single band.

There are many variations of the origin of this lore, and the moon handpicked her favourite one for me. She propped herself against a black wall and narrated, in a soft voice, the story of two fish called the Ichthyes. These fish daringly pushed an egg onto the shore of the Euphrates River. Their efforts birthed Aphrodite—the Greek goddess of love and beauty. The Ichthyes were rewarded with a place among the stars, where they belonged. In my reimagination, I gave these fish a place in the cove of two crescent moons.

I will use countless sun-moon analogies until I finally cave in and admit it's time to move on. *I will shine in the cove of two crescent moons, where the sun's light cannot reach me.*

There are some lines I have blurred, others I have crossed, and many I have been afraid to draw. Despite these myriad lines cutting through my moons, I will reclaim my Piscean identity. And, with it, I will find the confidence to write new chapters in the book of my life. Perhaps, that is why I chose to memorialise this reminder so close to my heart.

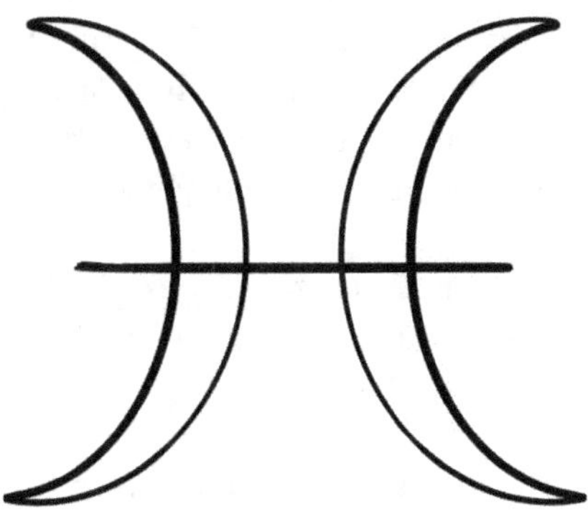

Unst(art)ed

If you're an artist, this is your reminder that you don't owe anyone your thoughts, feelings, and stories. It's not your responsibility to pour your heart out, just to fill someone else's void. Creating something for your own freedom of expression isn't selfish; *it's cathartic.*

The pretentious poems you wrote after your first heartbreak—yes, the ones that made you cringe when you stumbled upon them on a random Tuesday afternoon—are all yours to keep. Treasure them. They may seem insignificant now, but honestly, your words were all you had at one point. They are the reason you can laugh about what once made you cry.

The most compelling book was possibly discarded without ever having a second reader.

The most brilliant mural was probably tainted by *paan*[1] and urine, not protected by varnish.

The most soulful song was likely composed by an underground rapper without access to a studio.

---

1   A food item consisting of betel leaves wrapped around a mixture that could include areca nuts, lime, tobacco, or other flavouring ingredients. In this context, 'taint' refers to the marks or stains left behind when people chew *paan* and subsequently spit it out.

Perhaps, the most promising artists think and create in dialects native to their own hometowns, far from the colonial inheritance of English or other widely spoken languages. And one day, their unique work might get translated and reborn—*or not.*

> My favourite artists
> create their legacies
> in secret cellars,
> drawing on their hidden talents
> to please no one in particular.

There are a million artists who channel their energy through a million mediums. But one thing unites us all: the fear of taking the very first step. Some overcome it. Others let it confine them. For the longest time, I let it trap me within horizontal bars. But now, I have embraced the essence of *art for art's sake.*

There are numerous paths we can take to spread empathy and compassion. Giving away the most tortured and vulnerable parts of ourselves is one way, but it is not the only way.

> Sometimes, those parts have clipped wings that are not ready to see the light of day. Let them fester in the dark caves of your body, lest they take after Icarus and fly too close to the sun.

When the people I wanted to run off into the sunset with, closed their curtains on me, I knew it was time for me to fly. I had to fly *alone*, just like the five alphabets in my name, which are coincidentally arranged in that order. I used my nest as a launch pad and jumped headfirst off the roof, hoping that I would soar. And I did.

I'm unsure just how long I can use analogies of birds and azure skies to visualise hope. It's a cliché that, strangely enough, gives me...hope. Hope to step out of the comfort of my blanket. Hope to envelop the world in my warmth. Hope to make someone else feel safe. And so, I continue to hope.

I hope you find it in yourself to tell your truth, your side of the story, and your hopes as they are. If not, please promise me that you will keep a secret between us: *you are my favourite secret artist.*

My Bengali Grandmother

Dear Shuddu *masi[1]*,

Mom says that you joined our family eight years before I was born. You were her caretaker back in Kolkata but grew into a role where you raised my sister and me. In fact, I accepted you as my grandmother long before I could talk.

Strangely, I find it challenging to translate this letter into your native language. You swallowed your own language to communicate in mine; you found it unfair for an infant to stretch themselves beyond their crib.

Your broken Hindi sounded as mesmerising as Urdu poetry.

Do you remember how much I used to love your touch? You would caress my round cheeks and tell me how beautiful it was to have roses on my face when everyone else plucked them like over-ripened tomatoes.

Do you remember my essay on the cultural connotations of recipes for my Anthropology assignment last year? I wrote about your spicy *aloo dum[2]* recipe and how Yamini

---

1   In Hindi, *masi* is an endearing term used to describe one's mother's sister. However, in this context, Shuddu *masi* is not related to me by blood.

2   *Aloo* is the Hindi word for potatoes, while *dum* refers to the cooking process in which the potatoes are slow-cooked with steam. Subsequently, the potatoes are fried and simmered in a rich gravy, which typically consists of a blend of various spices, tomatoes, onions, and sometimes yoghurt or cream.

and I documented it during the lockdown. This way, it would stay with us forever.

I wish you could have stayed with us forever.

I long to sit by your side, whether it be in the kitchen, the living room, or anywhere else. You possessed this magical power to transform the ground beneath your feet into castles of love. In your presence, dragons became my friends, and ordinary moments transformed into legends to be recounted for aeons. Today, you are my superhero, and I want to cherish the stories we wrote together.

One of my favourite memories is when you would drop me off at the bus stop each morning and pick me up each afternoon. In the meantime, you bonded with all the other children because you had a knack for spreading warmth and love. Even on the basketball court, you would try to bounce the ball and join in as if you were a child.

> When the deck was stacked against me, you turned it into a pack of UNO cards and encouraged me to play.

I used to stockpile sheets of stickers, saving them for something 'perfect' because they felt too permanent to waste. Then, one day, you peeled them off and placed them on my nails—my first set of acrylics. You also surprised me with a pinwheel in one hand, a balloon in the other, and pure love in both.

Thank you for shielding me by keeping harm at arm's length. Everyone thinks I'm too young to remember, *but I only wish I could forget.* I wish I could forget the feeling of waiting with bated breath, unsure when the next war would erupt and cause bombs to go off. But in a space marred by hypervigilance, you were the reason for my happiness.

When I got older, your palms retained their healing power. They were like traditional bandages—a remedy for everything—whether it was a stubbed toe against the sharp edge of a table or the heartbreaks that claimed my sleepless nights as their own. I remember how you sacrificed your *saris*[3] for me, letting my tears soil the cloth covering your lap. Being a teenager was stressful, but you untangled my knots with almond oil; *you braided blades of grass into my hair and let brown lilies bloom in them.*

> Your toothless grin and the wisdom woven into the silver strands of your slicked-back bun tell the story of a life that changed others.

I know I call you often, but not as often as I'd like. I think it saddens me to hear you say the English words I once taught you—"I love you and I miss you". My heart palpitates because I wonder if it will be the last time I hear your voice or see your face in a little box. It pains me to watch you age: walking slowly instead of jogging alongside me, and taking bi-weekly dialysis treatments instead of the medicines mom would sort out for you.

---

3   A *sari* is a traditional attire worn by women in South Asian countries. It is a long piece of fabric that is elegantly draped around the body. It is also complemented with a matching blouse and a petticoat (underskirt).

I want you to visit our new home, so the walls can see the phenomenal woman I've been telling them about all these years. I want to serve you a hot meal and watch you list the spices I used, off the top of your head. Only you have the power to step onto the floor where gravity pulls me down on dark days, and lift me up again. Please will you enter my bedroom?

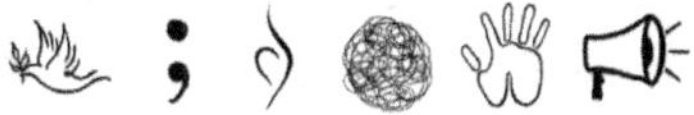

Dear Bulimia,

I will no longer allow you to bully me. You have cast your net over my sea of security and pulled it right out of my throat, far too many times, for far too long.

You knew how much I loved romance novels, so you made me fall truly, madly, deeply in love with you. We became a Stockholm Syndrome story, years in the making: you, my mysterious captor, and I, your awestruck hostage.

You held me so tight that it felt like I couldn't breathe, but that's love, right?

Love makes your heart skip beats and your stomach miss meals, right?

Time slipped away as you spent every spare second wolfing me down in an intimate entwinement. I became consumed by your fervour. Our attachment at the hip was symbolic of the magazine cutout on my wall—'A *moment on the lips, a lifetime on the hips'*.

We were supposed to have our forever, right?
But you left me tongue-tied and physically incapable of answering that question.

And yet, I still reminisce about all those games we used to play together. You would hide and I would seek, or

I would hide, but no one would attempt to find me. I
don't know if I would have defended you, had someone
noticed and asked why I was crouched inside a cabinet
with 25 packets of chips and a long line of ants to keep
me company.

You possessed an uncanny ability to convince everyone
that you were the one for me. They praised you to
the skies for making me float like a light, thin, stratus
cloud. You were the force behind my transformation,
guiding me to become a healthier and happier version
of myself. But did you truly achieve that?

The society that promises you
you are beautiful as you are,
is the same one that reflects you
in an illusive mirror
to gaze inward
and remind yourself
you're a sinner.

But dare you seek an altar
or sing along to the songs
your hip dips can play.

You are only programmed
to secretly weep
until you splinter
like shards of glass
with edges sharp enough
to prick you in your sleep.

As a child, I was told that my excessive weight could prove fatal. However, no one cautioned me about how the process of losing it could yield the same outcome. So, I didn't confide in anyone about the true nature of the beast you were. I didn't need help shedding weight—a subject on which everyone suddenly became an expert. But in making them proud of me, I let myself down.

You made me swallow everything but my own pride.

You stuffed me into the lifelong delusion that I should defile my body with lipstick smears and circle the parts that deserve to be chopped off behind closed doors.

You taught me that my body was not to be seen in public or loved in private.

In a nutshell,
I became the shell of a woman—
sand in my fragile hourglass
falling,
falling,
slowly
falling,
until I became as empty
as a warehouse
devoid of memories to keep.

You even made me envy your sister, Anorexia, who is no better than you are. The only difference is she made her unwanted presence felt and visible to others, so they could express their concern and support. But you were invisible and made me appear perfectly fine, if not perfect.

You masqueraded as my partner in crime, when you were really the murder weapon right under everyone's noses. In this *Silence of the Lambs* adaptation, you quietly took me away to your crime scene and gave in to the dreams society wished for me.

No more. Both of you are sick and twisted, and I am severing ties with your family. You feign empowering your victims and make us believe we hold the reins. In reality, you two are the puppeteers profiting off us— the headlining performers of your atrocious shows. We spread ourselves too thin for you. No. More. *We stand as survivors now.*

Today, I am as violent as you have been all these years.

You made me feel so small... in so many ways. You made me believe I wanted to be small. But I am freeing myself from your bizarre world of numbers and comparisons.

Will my descendants be concerned about the body fat percentage etched into my epitaph? Unlikely.

Will they long to discover whether I embodied kindness, honesty, and creativity? Probably.

And so, I don't want to spend my entire day trapped in a vicious cycle of running in circles. I am no longer an unsuspecting hamster on an electric wheel in a lab experiment. This time, I will outrun you. I will fuel my body with all the foods you once made me fear. Guilt will not engulf me if I do not wallow in self-pity; double negatives will be the only negatives in my life.

I will cinch my decision to occupy the weights section at a male-dominated gym and build the biggest, strongest version of myself. I will have the strength to thrust the weight of grown adults off my body and make up for all those times I physically could not.

I will also train to be confident in my own skin, regardless of how beautiful models on Instagram are, with their porcelain faces, skinny legs, and toned abs. I am slowly learning that their beauty does not take away from mine; we can co-exist. In any case, beauty is not the social currency I will use to buy validation.

My name, Salonee, may mean 'beautiful', but I don't have to succumb to the pressure that was imposed on me the moment I was born. I won't seek accommodations in places where I don't fit in; instead, I'll celebrate the ones that welcome me with arms as open as my heart.

> When Lana Del Rey sang, "Will you still love me when I'm no longer young and beautiful?", it felt like a question my body posed to me.

Except I don't feel beautiful even at this young age, despite all the filters, angled posing, and curated lies that find truth on my phone. After all, *'Nothing tastes as good as skinny feels'* graced the covers of the magazines I read growing up. Cellulite, texture, acne, and fat rolls were all seamlessly erased with digital brushes. I believed that if I possessed any of these, I was unworthy of love. And if someone did claim to love me, they were lying. They were not *actually* attracted to me; they settled for me out of sheer pity.

> Empty calories
> from sticky sweets,
> and empty promises
> from sticky-sweet compliments,
> will not send blood
> rushing down my cheeks.

My resistance enrages you, doesn't it? I can feel you scheming for revenge; we are cut from the same cloth. You still make me miss out on social events and trips because my body doesn't look 'thin enough'. You still infiltrate my kitchen on the days when my emotions obscure my rationality. You still push me towards my mirror, seize my eyelids, and extract tears from my dehydrated soul.

In these moments, I see the scared, overweight little girl who used to wonder why everyone was shouting at her. I remember being brutally beaten up and bullied for being too fat, the memories of which haunt me to this day. I recall how I was told to "close my dustbin mouth because there was already so much trash stuffed in it" or compared to slimmer girls who would find romantic partners in ways I never could. Those words hurt me then, and they continue to sting me even today.

Therapy can only be effective if I let go of the past, but how do I do that? Even after shedding the weight I was pressured to lose, that little girl still lives inside me. She still tries to communicate just how rejected, ugly, and lonely she feels, but I shut her out and neglect her needs—much like others used to do.

> Out of all the people I owe an apology to, *she deserves the biggest one.*

But not you. It all started and ended with you before I even knew your name. My brain isn't wired for mathematics, yet you made me sum up calories and subtract every shred of joy. You forced me to track every meal I ate, every step I took, everything that should have felt 'normal'...only to get nowhere.

> They say the journey is better than the destination.
> But here, neither of them seems worth the pain.

I am throwing this calculator out the window, along with all those magazines, scales, tapes, and other numbers that dictated how many inches I needed to alter, or how happy I was allowed to be. And you know, what? I will change, and I will be happy. *Just watch me.*

> I have been talking about wanting to take up space these days. And so, my voice will fill up pages and pages: with insecurity and confidence, hostility and calm, love and hate, all at once.

This is your formal notice that your unwilling tenant is vacating the premises. I have paid excess rent for a

shoddy studio apartment on the bad side of town, far
too many times, for far too long. The bill for my final
month is prepaid, so don't contact me anymore. Also, I
must tell you, I've warned all those in search of a home,
to steer clear of yours. I'm not sorry about that. In fact,
I'm not sorry about *anything*.

Oh, and lastly, don't sit by the telephone, waiting for
me to send you any more voicemails. I'm hanging up on
you for good. *Goodbye for good.*

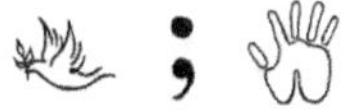

Vulnerability

I never learned to swim,
so I'll drown in a pool
of my own blood,
gasping for breath
until my lungs fail,
and my heart stops,
and I can't hear
the whistle of the cops.

I'll close my eyes
and let the darkness
wed my lifeless corpse—
a bride who could not bear
to witness the sight
of a girl so loved
hate herself so much.

If there's one thing I've embraced wholeheartedly, it's my vulnerability. My heart has overflowed with emotions for as long as I can remember. I feel so deeply that I can either sink into the bottomless ocean of my thoughts or cut through it agilely and gracefully.

But these two survival instincts have wreaked havoc in a mind I don't recognise.

Sometimes, my thoughts get dangerously loud. They bang on rusty doors, screaming for me to let them out, promising they'll make everything okay. They say they'll finally stop reliving the abuse my body remembers, but my brain doesn't; ultimately, *the body keeps the score*[1].

But there is no lighthouse or lifeguard in sight. There is no anchor to ground their flow.

What if they slip through my fingers like sand, making me lose all power over them? What if they are the Loch Ness monster I secretly make them out to be? What if they protrude from the water, betray my trust, and kill the people who make me feel alive?

I have been seeking definitive answers but found none on the shores. Perhaps, they lie in the sea, floating and trapped in a bottle: a make-believe world of happiness and love waiting to be discovered.

But when I went searching for that message in a bottle, the only glass that I found on the beach was the one that gashed my ankle. It was then that I realised I had been standing in quicksand.

I, a water sign, can never fathom the signs on the water. I suppose accidentally drowning as a child does that to you. I suppose intentionally wanting to drown as an adult does that to you. Swimming is not a sport I enjoy dabbling in, unless it has undertones of Greek mythology.

"Poseidon, when will you strike me with your trident? I beckon you to ingest me, but you silence me with your thrashing waves. You tantalise and mock me, *letting the water flow over my toes, but never my entire body.*"

---

1   This is a reference to the book *The Body Keeps the Score: Mind, Brain and Body in the Transformation of Trauma* by Bessel van der Kolk.

I don't think these feelings make me any less of a person, or any less worthy of the love I deserve.

Of the same kindness and warmth I send out
into the universe.

Of the entire solar system delicately planting
a kiss on my cheek when I believe there is no
light left in me.

The same hostility that makes me fight, makes me fight for my loved ones. The same stubbornness that renders me almost incapable of change, makes me fiercely loyal. The same jealousy that makes me want to shed my skin to be 'that girl', makes me respect her. All of these things make me want to improve myself, and yet, somehow, also accept myself.

But why can't you accept yourself?

If you can admire the luminosity of the Kepler, why can't you see the way your face glows when sunlight streams into your bedroom through the sheer curtains? You shine, just like celestial bodies do. *Do not let the mundane dim your inherent ethereality.*

You know, I used to fear that I had sailed past the edge of normality with no return ticket. I was prepared to let my thoughts linger between my oar and me, as I rowed by myself. After all, most people who have braved storms, don't let long-gone memories of the tempest affect them.

But I catastrophise everything.
Every. Little. Thing.

I am a lot. I am an overwhelming presence, but I am also an artist whose creative juices flow into TetraPaks. I am an overthinking crybaby, but I am also a wistful dreamer. I am also full of forgiveness and a hundred chances for others and myself. I am black and white and morally grey.

Is that good? Is that bad? Is it somewhere in between? Once again, I don't have the answers.

But I do know that losing me is losing a lot.
And I wear that like my heart on my sleeve.

Inner Child

To the little girl who is a shell of me,

I am sorry for not loving you and letting you accept lovelessness as your reality.

You don't know this yet, but isolating yourself will soon become a visceral memory. And when you try to scream for help, your body won't choose between fight or flight; it will simply go numb.

I am sorry for not thawing your freeze trauma response.

I have so many things to apologise to you for, but right now, you don't need apologies. You need the strength to believe that everything will be okay. Now, I cannot promise that everything will be completely okay, but I can say that the future has beautiful things in store for you.

So, each time you're alone, scribbling away in a feeble attempt to assemble shards of glass you didn't break, know that the bad will pass. The bruises on your flesh and heart will fade. You'll learn that your sensitivity, honesty, and emotionality are all part of your peaceful arsenal; *they are your ultimate power.*

I am living proof that you'll find reasons to live, often in the most unexpected places and with the loveliest people.

You'll discover that your favourite film is *Dead Poets Society,* based on a recommendation from a long-gone partner, for whom you'll always have a soft spot. You'll write poems about another lover—one you still cherish—because he was good to you in ways that felt unfamiliar.

You'll learn to let go of the people who left and focus on those who chose to stay.

You'll hold teachers closer to your heart than peers during your school years. They will nurture your love for writing, and you'll thank them for it years after graduation. In university, you'll find your chosen family who love you for who you are. This might feel unrealistic because the first two years of university will mentally destroy you. However, by the third year, you'll step into a life filled with love that surpasses your wildest imagination.

You'll forge a deeper connection with your parents and realise that they value and support you in the smallest ways every single day. Your father will answer every call on the first ring, and your mother will become your favourite confidante. Your sisters will be your biggest cheerleaders, and you'll wish you had the words to tell them just how much you treasure them.

You'll try, be, and do many things. But the void that begs for accomplishment, praise, and other forms of external validation, will be filled by failure.

You'll struggle to grasp mathematics and abandon it in the eighth grade. An autorickshaw will unexpectedly slam into your bicycle, toppling you over and resulting in multiple stitches. You'll walk on broken eggshells just to clear the path for other people. Your boyfriend will slow dance with his best friend, and you'll watch how close their faces are in a video on social media. Yet, you'll never confront him about it because you'll already have labelled yourself as crazy and insecure.

You'll internalise images of your body type as an entity of disdain. You'll repeat mistakes and engage in self-sabotaging behaviours that undermine your own happiness. All of this is part of the process of shedding layer after layer to discover the one you wish to preserve.

I'm here to remind you that you can set aside this multitude of ambitions for a while. You don't need to assume the roles of a poet, artist, musician, athlete, photographer, lover, daughter, sister, or anyone else. You are allowed to exist independently, for your own sake.

And yet, you can proudly embrace the title of a writer to define your identity. Unfortunately, this label will become tainted by others' expectations of what a writer 'looks' or 'writes' like. You'll lose touch with writing, and instead, redefine your safe space by finding new places to grow.

Saying goodbye can be scary, but it can also be healing.

Temporarily stepping away from writing will enable you to find catharsis at the gym. You'll join a beautiful and supportive community that encourages you to be the best version of yourself. And yes, you'll work out to be stronger, not to please someone who is pushing you to shrink into a smaller body. In fact, you'll stop caring about whether the aesthetics of your body please others at all. You'll only care about endorphin rushes, setting new records for yourself, and seeing the same people with the kindest hearts, for two hours every day. *The place that once frightened you, will slowly become your home.*

But oh, writing will find its way back to you.

Your first safe space will wrap you in its arms when you need it the most. Its warm, familiar embrace will show you that hands harbour love. Unlike myself or anyone else, writing will never let you down. Trust that writing will help you process everything you are going through, but are unable to understand right now. The absence of clarity at this moment is because it will all make sense in due course. These experiences will mould you into an individual who cares deeply, makes tremendous efforts, and loves hard.

You'll reach out to me, not just today, but on numerous occasions. Please remember that, even when you feel isolated, you are not truly alone. In some parallel dimension, I am right there, holding your hand, and sharing cheesecake with you. Here, we are watching planes take off and land from the terrace of our building. In these planes, you'll discover poetry, and soon, you'll see poetry everywhere.

You'll retain three letters from the word 'heartbreak'—*art*.

You'll find purpose in giving back to society and apply for a social justice fellowship to work with students in government schools. I can't tell you how it will turn out because I have not yet embarked on this journey, but I have a feeling that it will be a humbling and extraordinary one. I believe that the students will teach me more than I can teach them. I would love to introduce you to these children. But before you meet them, we will collaborate on a project together. This is something you'll dream about all your life.

But you'll decide it is time to wake up only on the day you almost don't.

The ink that leaks from your eyes will not evaporate from your pages; instead, it will invite the inkwells in others' eyes to embrace vulnerability. These pages will form a book that bears the weight of your life. You'll write entirely for yourself, but even then, someone will borrow your poems to construct the rooftop of their new shelter.

The heartbeat of your work will forever beat to the drum of your unwavering passion.

We did it. We really did it this time around. We chiselled away at our insecurities and carved out the confidence to share our stories. Do you remember the stone where you once engraved the pain that seemed insurmountable? My girl, that very stone is now your beautifully uncomfortable legacy. *You* did it.

Forevermore

Under gothic arches
and cobblestone pathways,
where the winds,
for 154 years,
have blown,
I found the only love
I've ever really known.

Linking arms with them at an overcrowded train station. Relentlessly teasing them about being late for every class. Editing their essays while they *try* to teach you statistics in the library. Bonding over having the same favourite font, out of all possible nerdy interests. Dreaming about the Broadway productions you aspire to watch one day.

Scanning each other from top to bottom to find specific fashion elements to compliment. Introducing each other to new food in the canteen. Stopping to pet all the cats in sight. Claiming the woods in your college as your own. Absorbing the gentle breeze that rustles the leaves of the tree against which you both rest, reading classics together.

Feeling a warm glow in your heart each time you sense their presence.

Dancing to a song you've never heard before, solely because it's their favourite. Playing Dandiya[1] in *lehengas*[2] and sneakers. Belting out overrated songs by mainstream musicians with hairbrushes in front of a bathroom mirror. Scrawling matching tattoos on your forearms using ballpoint ink. Slyly stealing their Monopoly money when they leave the room to grab a snack.

Snuggling with more people than a single blanket can fit. Taking turns sharing stories, only to have each story intermingled with a million other unrelated ones. Spotting a baby lizard near their pillow and warning (read: startling) them about its existence while they are half-conscious. Watching them laugh so hard that they involuntarily flail around and smack your knees.

Discovering the pureness of friendship for the very first time.

Engaging in deep conversations about life while spontaneously cycling 30 kilometres at 4:00 a.m. Having secret sleepovers on the rocks by the seaside. Keeping each other awake to watch the sunrise, only to realise you're facing the wrong direction. Embarking on road trips to their hometown and immersing yourself in their childhood memories.

Surprising them with their favourite flower after stumbling upon it at a roadside stall. Baking them

[1]   A traditional Indian folk dance that originates from the state of Gujarat, Dandiya is usually performed during a nine-day festival called Navaratri. Some of its characteristic features entail using ornate wooden sticks called *dandiyas* and dancing in circular formations.
[2]   A traditional Indian ankle-length skirt, usually worn by women during ceremonial events.

vegan cheesecake to demonstrate your support for their activism. Expressing sincere curiosity about their most recent passion. Sharing your gym playlist and workout split with them because they're unsure where to begin.

Running marathons, *not sprints.*

Writing lengthy essays of appreciation. Responding with equally lengthy replies to those appreciative essays. Composing a collaborative poem for a literary publication on their terrace, fuelled by ice cream and a shared passion for dark poetry. Being reminded that *The Boy, the Mole, the Fox and the Horse* can still be one of your favourite books, even if you've associated it with your ex-boyfriend who never returned your annotated copy of it.

Seeing them contribute to the deafening roar of "GO SAL!" during your first open mic after a four-year break. Falling in love with writing again because they recounted, time and time again, how reading your pieces made them *feel* something.

Caring so deeply for them that they know they'll always have a home in you, and you, in them.

Knowing they trust you with their darkest thoughts. Rubbing your thumb against theirs when you feel their breath becoming unsteady. Always having pocket tissues on hand, just in case. Letting their snot soak your hair. Actively listening to their hauntingly traumatic experiences. Showing up for them when no one else does. Crying tears of despair and distraught and delight, all at once. Empowering them so often, they forget they were ever insecure in the first place. Reassuring them they deserve better than a mediocre man who dog-eared the lines on their palms, only to put down the book of their relationship.

Holding it together when friends who mean the
world to you, move half the world away.

Controlling your own tears so they don't cry—then collapsing into each other's arms and holding on tight as if it's not goodbye. Knowing that last hug silently shelters a million stories. Writing farewell letters to usher in a new era. Carrying little pieces of them in dainty pendants and borrowed crop tops. Coordinating breakfast-dinner dates over FaceTime because you're in different time zones.

Living in a world where they hold onto their promises like the words are engraved in your virtually intertwined fingers. Sharing your biggest dreams with them, and waking up to all of them coming true. Imagining your future children becoming best friends and growing up together, while you grow old together.

It's worth putting death on hold
to watch this wrinkle in time[3]
come to life one day.

3   This is a subtle nod to *A Wrinkle in Time,* a science fantasy novel written by Madeleine L'Engle. It was one of my favourite stories growing up.

To everyone who saw themselves
in my musings about our memories,

I am uncertain about many things, but there is
one thing I can say with certainty—
the sweater of our bond will forever be close-knit.

I know this because I have fallen in love with so many
people, so many times, only to realise...

This is the balm that soothes each sore.

This is the symphony of happiness,
enveloping me to my core.

This is the love that whispers tenderly,
even on distant shores,
"I love you forevermore."

To All the Letters I Never Sent

When I check for lumps,
I never touch my throat
or the thorns adorning
my unfinished notes.

I injured my back while deadlifting two weeks ago. It has been difficult to bend, turn, and perform other basic tasks. Even the TENS treatment, which the physiotherapist assured me would alleviate the strain, made me uncomfortable.

But you wouldn't know. How could you? *I didn't write a letter about it.*

Although it was physically painful, I have realised that I only put pen to paper for the aches that mentally demolish me. If my suffering had persisted for another week, perhaps you would have received a letter. But I'm doing better now.

You know that I've written and personally hand-delivered many letters to many people: my mother, my best friend, past lovers, and even myself. Yet, I have shed the most tears over you and how I had to destroy you; it was the only way to move on from the stories I told you in confidence.

I didn't know if you would betray me; *I never gave you the chance to try.*

All I knew was that I couldn't bear the weight of the words I poured into you. I empathised with a mother who deserted her child, gulping down the guilt of knowing she could not care for her own.

Hypocrisy seems to be a recurring motif within my words and veins, *flowing off me and seeping into you.*

It's funny that I blabber about people leaving when I'm the one who left you first. You're the letters that should've been shipped off first thing in the morning: stamped, sealed, and ready to travel the world. The kind that birds carry between their beaks with a sense of urgency, as the winds follow familiar routes on their wings.

They should've flown you straight to freedom, and, by extension, *set me free too.*

But you know Fear lives behind a locked door in my mind, masquerading as a façade of safety and certainty. Fear is the only friend who has stayed all my life, and one I cannot attempt to outgrow as I did with Anger.

I've written undispatched letters to Fear too. But my words often fail to make sense, for Fear delicately balances herself on my signature purple gel pen, whispering sweet nothings to me.

She cackles as she watches how I struggle to decipher my own emotions. She drones on in my ears that my writing will never be moving enough for her to cry. She drives me insane when I need to write her letters, night after night, just to find a fragment of sanity.

Fear starves me of salvation.

I think she always will.

But this time, *all my letters will stay.*

You Are
a Poet

I believe that everyone has a story to tell. But when your mind struggles to let you survive, you cannot tell those stories. *You become those stories.* You carry them in your eyes and invite a few people to meet your gaze.

I would love for you to use this space to jot down your stories:

The ones you barely even remember.

The ones you don't want to share because they paint you in a 'bad' light.

The ones you want to share but are afraid no one will believe.

Whatever your stories are, you can tell them, even if only to yourself. Here's how:

Step One: You can interpret the chapter titles as you like and choose your stories. You can grip the nib of your pen, the tip of your paintbrush, or use any other medium that brings you joy.

Step Two: You can doodle a sketch, write a letter, draft a storyboard, or stick photographs and turn this into a scrapbook. You can also peruse my poems and make your own blackout poetry from them. Whatever you do, I hope it repairs your heart.

Step Three (optional): You can remove all traces of your stories from existence. Feel free to tear off your melodramatic monologues and toss them straight into the dustbin.

There is strength in quiet resilience. You have many beautiful chapters hidden in the layers under your skin. So, on the days you do not feel like a poet, an artist, or any other title you wish you could use to define yourself, please remember that *you are a living story.*

Of Loss *and Learning*

Of Love *and Healing*

Of Letters *and Musings*

Thank you for staying till the end.

From one storyteller to another.

Acknowledgements

Authors are often advised to keep their acknowledgements section concise. However, as a proponent of long-form poetry, I do not believe that brevity equates to quality. So, please bear with me as I express my gratitude to many people for various reasons; their meaningful contributions deserve appropriate credit.

To my parents,
Thank you for encouraging me to unapologetically follow my passions. Mom, you have fought wars and made sacrifices for me every step of the way. I hope to imbibe your kindness, generosity, and resilience. Dad, thank you for being my pillar of support and helping me discover 'The Magic Within'. Our Sunday visits to Crossword and Shemaroo are the happiest memories of my childhood. I attribute my love for storytelling entirely to you.

To Yamini and Ankita,
I wish there was a single word that could fully convey the depth of my gratitude for having sisters who have defined unconditional love for me. Thank you for standing by me during my most challenging moments, and for celebrating me during my most joyful ones. You embody the essence of the Divine Feminine and show me what it genuinely means to be a family.

To Shuddu masi,
Thank you for raising me to be strong and compassionate like you. I miss you every day.

To my aunts and uncles,
It amuses me that you still joke about how I, as a little child, exclaimed that I wanted to win the Nobel Prize for Literature. Although a far-fetched dream, you were the first people to tell me that you could not wait to read my book. Billu masi, Arun, Rekha masi, Matthew, Mimi, and Chhotu mama—I owe all of you, my second parents, so much.

To my cousins,
Ritika, Vinita, Ashwyn, and Anish bhaiya, thank you for being the most caring people who have showered me with affection all my life. I could not have made it this far without you.

To Siddhant,
I have grown up respecting and admiring you. Thank you for being someone I can count on and learn from in any situation.

To Adi,
There is no one I trust more than you to understand my inane epiphanies and safeguard my deepest, darkest secrets. Thank you for showing me what it feels like to have a best friend, brother, and lifelong partner in crime, all in one.

To Khushali,
You have been the loudest cheerleader dancing with pom-poms outside my window, telling me I could do it since day one. Your perennial river of thoughtful gestures and words of affirmation flows through my valley and makes it beautiful.

To Anushka,
From the day I conceptualised this book, I had hoped you would illustrate it. You have patiently listened to my galaxy of ideas and gracefully brought my vision for each planet to life. For that and all that you silently do for everyone you love, thank you.

To Rashi,
I have been in awe of your work ethic and amiable personality since we first discussed Sociology and Anthropology assignments three years ago. Thank you for coming on board and seamlessly weaving the most creative layout designs I have ever seen. Above all else, thank you for being so understanding and tolerating my *endless* revisions of the same content.

To my friends from college,
Jasmine, Devansh, Meghna, Shelly, Mehr, Sakshi, Aryan, Shafeen, Rashmi, and Janhavi, I am incredibly grateful for the special moments we have shared together. These moments have now become core memories that will always stay with me. "*I love you forevermore.*"

To my focus group,
Thank you for contributing your opinions during the final stage of editing for *I Am Not a Poet*. This version of the book could not have existed without your valuable feedback and unwavering faith in me.

To Tuhina and Suraj,
You came through for me when I started losing hope that my dream would ever become a reality. Thank you for helping me rebuild my crumbled castle, one metaphorical brick at a time.

To my English teachers from school,
I want to express my heartfelt gratitude to each of you
for believing in my capabilities when I first stepped into
the world of words. Ms Fernandes, Ms Golwala, Ms
D'Souza, and Ms Pawar, you deserve immense credit for
your role in shaping generations of thinkers, dreamers,
and artists.

To Viky sir and Dimple ma'am,
Your presence in my life extended far beyond the role
of tuition teachers. Thank you for gently guiding me
to push my limits and carve beautiful possibilities for
myself.

To the people I have loved and lost,
Thank you for being part of my story and allowing
me to write chapters in yours. The memories we
created together hold a special place in my heart, and I
appreciate you for imparting valuable lessons that I will
carry forward with me. Although our paths may have
taken different directions, I wish for your journey to be
filled with love, peace, and contentment.

To my readers,
This book is mere paper without you to breathe life
and meaning into the words. I am deeply humbled and
honoured by your support. Together, we have brought
this project to fruition. I hope you think of *I Am Not a
Poet* as a warm and inviting home; its doors will always
be open for you whenever you need a safe space.

About the Team

Author and Illustrator

Salonee Kumar (she/her) is a Social-Emotional Learning (SEL) Fellow at Apni Shala Foundation, a non-profit organisation based in Mumbai, India. This fellowship programme lies at the intersection of education and mental health, with the goal of nurturing SEL competencies among students living in systemic poverty. In addition to her work in municipal schools, she is leading a Field Action Research Project on intergenerational storytelling rooted in Narrative Practices.

She holds a Bachelor of Arts (B.A.) degree in Psychology from St. Xavier's College in Mumbai. She is also an alumna of Bombay Scottish School, Mahim, in Mumbai. She is an awardee of the Times Scholars 2019-20 scholarship from The Times of India and a Certificate of Merit (Top 15) for the Hindustan Times Essay Scholarship 2016-17.

During her formative years, Salonee found solace and expression in art, particularly through writing and sketching. She has since published numerous academic articles and creative pieces. She wrote the content and conceptualised the artwork for her debut book, *I Am Not a Poet,* at the age of 21. Through her projects, she aims to advocate for trauma-informed and queer-affirmative mental healthcare, body neutrality, suicide prevention, intersectional feminism, and social justice, among other pressing issues.

Her hobbies entail strength training at the gym, mentally adopting every stray animal she sees, and curating *ridiculously* long playlists.

Illustrator

Anushka Dey (she/her) is a Mumbai-based Human Resources personnel with a Bachelor of Arts (B.A.) degree in Psychology from St Xavier's College in Mumbai. Her professional work centres on applying Industrial and Organisational Psychology principles to Learning and Development projects, and she strives to understand human behaviour in an organisational context.

Her hobbies include fine arts like graphite sketching, clay modelling, oil, watercolour, and fabric painting, as well as fibre arts like crochet, sewing, and embroidery. She is an avid reader, occasionally writing and performing poetry, with published work in *Women Empowerment Through Poetry* by the University of Mumbai.

Her art draws inspiration from the people and world around her, and she aims to use art as a healing medium that conveys the message 'You are not alone'. Recurring motifs in her pieces include themes of feminism, mental health, fantasy and folklore, and elements from the work of Renaissance and Impressionist artists.

I Am Not a Poet marks her venture into digital art, where she executed the illustrations in a manner that was in line with the author's vision: rough, messy, and perfectly imperfect. She hopes that the art accompanying the content will stay with the readers for a long time to come.

Layout Designer

Rashi Shah (she/her) is a design student currently pursuing her Bachelor of Design (B.Des.) degree at the National Institute of Design , Assam, India. Her creative journey is centred around illustration, typography, and publication design, where she passionately explores the art of visual storytelling and communication.

With a strong passion for design and a commitment to learning, Rashi is dedicated to improving her skills and understanding how design influences communities and cultures.

Originally from Mumbai and currently based in Jorhat, Assam, Rashi draws inspiration from her surroundings as she explores its rich culture and diverse landscapes. She believes that design has the power to bridge gaps, evoke emotions, and leave a lasting impact, and she aspires to contribute meaningfully to the world through her creative endeavours.

You can find her on Instagram @rashi_tries—her creative dump ground, a perpetual work in progress.

www.ingramcontent.com/pod-product-compliance
Lightning Source LLC
Chambersburg PA
CBHW050332160726
48002CB00001B/277